PASSIONS OF THE SOUL

T0120414

In memory of Metropolitan Kallistos of Diokleia,
mentor and pastor; and for John Stansfield,
steadfast friend.

PASSIONS OF THE SOUL

ROWAN WILLIAMS

BLOOMSBURY CONTINUUM
LONDON • OXFORD • NEW YORK • NEW DELHI • SYDNEY

BLOOMSBURY CONTINUUM
Bloomsbury Publishing Plc
50 Bedford Square, London, WC1B 3DP, UK
29 Earlsfort Terrace, Dublin 2, Ireland

BLOOMSBURY, BLOOMSBURY CONTINUUM and the Diana logo
are trademarks of Bloomsbury Publishing Plc

First published in Great Britain 2024

Copyright © Rowan Williams 2024

Rowan Williams has asserted his right under the Copyright, Designs
and Patents Act, 1988, to be identified as Author of this work

All rights reserved. No part of this publication may be reproduced or
transmitted in any form or by any means, electronic or mechanical,
including photocopying, recording, or any information storage or
retrieval system, without prior permission in writing from the publishers

Bloomsbury Publishing Plc does not have any control over, or
responsibility for, any third-party websites referred to or in this book.
All internet addresses given in this book were correct at the time of
going to press. The author and publisher regret any inconvenience
caused if addresses have changed or sites have ceased to exist, but can
accept no responsibility for any such changes

A catalogue record for this book is available from the British Library

Library of Congress Cataloguing-in-Publication data has been
applied for

ISBN: PB: 978-1-3994-1568-2; eBook: 978-1-3994-1569-9;
ePDF: 978-1-3994-1565-1

2 4 6 8 10 9 7 5 3

Typeset by Deanta Global Publishing Services, Chennai, India
Printed and bound in Great Britain by CPI Group (UK) Ltd,
Croydon CR0 4YY

To find out more about our authors and books visit
www.bloomsbury.com and sign up for our newsletters

CONTENTS

FOREWORD

The first part of this little book began as a series of retreat addresses given to the Anglican Benedictine community at Holy Cross Convent in Leicestershire some years ago. These were recorded by the community and made more widely available online by the kindness of Mucknell Abbey in Worcestershire. My old friend and former student Mark Barber generously volunteered to transcribe these, as he explains in his note below, so that I was able to edit them into a slightly more finished form; without his assistance and the care and intelligence he brought to the thankless labour of transcription, this book would not have been possible, and I am deeply grateful. But I must also record my warmest thanks to the Community of the Holy Cross and their Superior, Mother Mary Luke OSB, for their welcome and kindness, and to the Abbot and community of Mucknell for circulating the recordings. Robin Baird-Smith of Continuum was, as always, the soul of generous encouragement when the possibility of publishing these talks was first raised.

They are manifestly not designed as a scholarly discussion of the quite complex issues that are regularly raised by the interpretation of early Christian texts on the life of the spirit; but I hope to have given just enough by way of reference to indicate something of this substantial hinterland and the treatment of these questions by more seasoned experts. And I have also included two short essays aimed at a non-specialist readership, dealing with the context and character of early Christian thinking about the shape of moral and spiritual maturity, hoping that these may help to locate the discussion of the 'passions' against a background of wider developments in thinking about Christian identity and its distinctive language. No one in the earliest Christian communities thought in terms of a 'theology' developing alongside a 'spirituality'. What we see is an evolving *practice* (both communal and personal) that generated a variety of challenges to language, imagination and self-understanding. As has often been said, Christian doctrine took its distinctive shape only through reflection on the distinctiveness of how Christian women and men actually prayed.

That connectedness of doctrine and practice was deeply in evidence in the life of one of the greatest interpreters of the tradition in the English-speaking world, the late Metropolitan Kallistos of Diokleia, whose fusion of clarity in teaching and faithful witness in practice made an indelible impression on generations of students from all Christian confessions, myself included. I was fortunate enough to count him as a mentor and friend for over forty years, and his involvement, up to the very end of his life, in the translation and interpretation of the great Eastern anthology of guidance, the *Philokalia*, whose fifth and final volume appeared just as his life was drawing to its close, will be a permanent source of grace and inspiration. This book is dedicated jointly to his memory, and to a friend of the author and husband of the transcriber whose support has been material, unfailing and selfless.

Rowan Williams
Eastertide 2023
Cardiff

Note by Mark Barber

I first encountered Rowan in 1979 when, like my fellow Cambridge Theology undergraduates, I was somewhat startled by his saying a prayer before his lectures – God forbid!

Subsequently, he was my supervisor for a History of Theology paper in my second year, when I took essays to him once a week on a particular theologian such as Augustine – not knowing then that I was in the presence of a future authority on Augustine, Teresa of Ávila and a good few others.

We lost touch for nearly 40 years, during which I drifted into agnosticism and suffered a severe breakdown, taking me into a desert of the utmost aridity. Three years ago, when reading a passage in his book *God with Us*, I was sprung from that desert into pools of living water – 'the water that I shall give him shall be in him a well of water springing up to eternal life' (John 4.14).

'Oh, how often I remember the living water of which the Lord spoke to the woman of Samaria ... I used often to beseech the Lord to give me that water' (Teresa, *The Life*, ch.30). And 'In order to possess what you do not possess you must go by the way of dispossession' ('East Coker', TS Eliot quoting St John of the Cross Ascent of Mount Carmel, 1.13). As Rowan said to me, paraphrasing St John of the Cross, 'The (dark) night (of the soul) is the process by which intelligence is transformed into trust, memory into hope and will into love. I think I used the analogy of the 'hourglass' shape of the night: our ordinary mental and emotional processes go into a sort of black hole and emerge into another "universe", where we are opened up to God afresh.'

I hope I now can say, with St Paul, that 'I am crucified with Christ: nevertheless I live; yet not I but Christ liveth in me; and the life which I now live in the flesh I live by the faith of the Son of God, who loved me and gave himself for me' (Galatians 2.20).

Since then Rowan and I have become close friends, not just teacher and pupil and, while not a giant of the spiritual life, I believe I have made some progress through prayer and reflection on Scripture and the great spiritual writers – particularly the Spanish mystics Teresa of Ávila and St John of the Cross.

And so I instantly recognized these talks on *apatheia* – freedom from the passions and its relation to the Beatitudes – as a profound distillation of spiritual wisdom, honed by years of personal reflection and pastoral experience. Rowan graciously agreed that I could transcribe these talks so that he could expand them into a book. May this book bring readers, as it has brought me, closer to the Most Sacred Heart of Jesus, from whose pierced side flow blood and water – the fountain of sacramental life in the Church.

Mark Barber
Michaelmas 2022
Banbury

INTRODUCTION: A TRADITION
FOR LEARNING FREEDOM

Books on 'spirituality' continue to proliferate, but
those living in the early Christian centuries would
probably not have known what exactly they were
meant to be about. For the Eastern monastic world,
certainly, there was a clear notion of what you might
need to know if you were going to embark on a
lifetime of trying to let your eyes be opened to God
and to the world; before you could sensibly or safely
plunge into the contemplation of the divine, you were
going to need some formation in self-knowledge and
in the capacity to relate to the rest of creation without
selfish illusions. This meant formation in diagnosing
the kinds of reaction that might trap you in negative,
delusory and destructive patterns of action, and for
this numerous texts were produced outlining the
tools for such diagnostic skill. They were never seen
as any kind of 'syllabus'. Some writers are careful
to say that enlightenment can come to the simple
and unselfconscious no less than to the anxious and
supposedly intelligent. But the consensus evidently
was that it helped to have an agreed framework

for thinking about the sort of person you needed to become if your contemplative journey Godwards was not going to be a self-indulgent quest for gratifying experiences.

The literature from the Eastern monastic world is substantial, extending from the aphorisms and anecdotes of the first generation of monks and nuns in the Egyptian desert to the more detailed and reflective letters and treatises of the centuries that followed. It is a literature that retains a high level of continuity and coherence across many generations – which is why the famous Greek eighteenth-century anthology the *Philokalia* can take it for granted that the texts it contains represent a more or less unbroken stream of practical teaching, not simply of ideas. And the reception of the work in the Balkans and Russia strongly suggested that the appeal of this teaching was by no means restricted to those in monastic vows; laypeople absorbed aspects of the 'philokalic' view of the human self, learning some life-giving scepticism about unexamined motivations and self-gratifying pietism. The vision of liberated action and perception in the texts remains a source of powerful critical perspective on the mechanisms of acquisitiveness, the myths of human autonomy and isolation from the material universe and the techniques of silencing or dehumanizing what challenges these myths and mechanisms. (And one of the bitterest ironies of our world at the moment is that one of the cultures most marked by these traditions, the world of Christian Russia, has been so comprehensively captured by the illusions most clearly identified in the philokalic texts.)

But there is no denying that the literature in question is not all that easy for a contemporary Western Christian to digest. The vocabulary can be puzzling, the devotional rhetoric may not be what we are used to and the quantity of material is considerable. What follows is a brief orientation to some elements of the traditional Eastern Christian approach to a certain kind of growth in self-awareness – what the texts themselves call 'wakefulness' – as a preliminary in the process of giving oneself to God in silence and loving God's creation in humility and truthfulness. It does no more than scratch the surface of a rich and complex legacy, but may perhaps open a door or two. And to help the reader find some more familiar points of connection I have proposed a way of reflecting on the diagnostic categories of the Eastern monastic tradition in relation to the Beatitudes announced by Jesus in the Gospel according to St Matthew. If these are a sketch of what a human life is like when lived in the awareness of God's Kingdom, the traditional analysis of the tumultuous 'passions of the soul', with their potential for both life and destructive or compulsive behaviour, may sharpen our sense of what stops us recognizing the Kingdom – its claim on us and its promise for us.

One of the great governing themes of early Christian spirituality is the concept represented by the word *apatheia*. Not a very good place to begin, it seems: the word sounds like 'apathy' – not surprisingly, since it is where our word comes from. And there is the first challenge in understanding. The idea that the goal of Christian life is to become completely apathetic may sound plausible to some people who have had unhappy experiences of Christian congregations, but this is not quite what the early monastic teachers meant by the word. Precisely because it plays such an enormous role in the spiritual understanding of the early Christians – and, to this day, of the Eastern Christian world – it seems worth our while to take some trouble to reflect on some of the great texts in which it figures, and to tease out the governing ideas that might make better sense of it.

We read, for example in some of these great early works,[1] that the state of *apatheia* is an anticipation of the resurrection.[2] We read that it is inseparable from love.[3] It is described as the essence of Christian liberty.[4] Here is a short passage from the sixth-century teacher Diadochos of Photike, which describes some of what is in mind when these early writers speak of *apatheia*:

> If, then, a man begins to make progress in keeping the commandments and calls ceaselessly on the Lord Jesus, the fire of God's grace spreads even to the heart's more outward organs of perception, consciously burning up the tares in the field of the soul. As a result, the demonic attacks cannot now penetrate to the depths of the soul, but can prick only that part of it which is subject to passion. When the ascetic has finally acquired all the virtues – and in particular the total shedding of possessions – then grace illuminates his whole being with a deeper awareness.[5]

Certainly not 'apathy': it's worth noticing how the ideal of freedom from 'passion' is connected here with a new level of awareness, a new clarity of vision. What these earlier writers of the Eastern spiritual tradition are talking about is regularly grounded in the idea that our habitual mental and spiritual condition is one in which we quite simply don't *see* clearly; and even in the Western tradition St Augustine will tell us that one of the effects of evil within us is that our minds are skewed. We don't know things as we ought to know them; we don't see things as we ought to see them. In these reflections we shall be trying to follow the way in which analysis of the passions in some of these texts can be read as something that opens the door to a clarifying of our vision, our perception, and to grasp more fully how this clarity of vision is what we need for our love to be *truthful*. That may not be a way of putting it that rings bells at first, but I want to focus on the idea of truthful love as a key to thinking about 'passion' and our liberation from it.

The texts we shall be thinking about are mostly from the extensive literature written in the eastern Mediterranean between about 450 and 750 CE, directed mostly (not exclusively) to people who were leading lives of seclusion in the monastic settlements of the region. One of the greatest exponents of contemplative practice in this period is the rather controversial figure of Evagrius of Pontus, who died in 399. Some of his ideas left his reputation under a cloud in the Greek-speaking churches, and his literary remains can be found in a number of unexpected places, preserved under the name of other writers, translated into languages other than Greek so that they have survived when the original Greek texts had been suppressed. In one significant piece of teaching he talks about the different ways in which we can see or know things around us. There is, he says, an 'angelic' way of seeing, a 'human' way and a 'diabolic' way. The angelic way of seeing things is seeing things just as they are, just as they emerge from the hand of God, we might say – an almost Zen-like clarity, perceiving the world in its simple thereness, resting on nothing but the creative act of God, glowing in its reality. The diabolic way of seeing the world is the opposite – the world of a kind of supermarket consumerism in which we experience and assess what is around us simply in terms of its profitability to us, as if it had no meaning except what our wants and fantasies projected on to it: never mind what it *is*, what can it do for *me*? And the 'human' way oscillates between these two, wobbling between the extremes, trying hard to see things straight but constantly slithering back into the self-referring mode of perception – stuffing the world into the bag of the ego.[6]

So, for someone like Evagrius, what we need to be working towards is the angelic way of seeing. Just to avoid misunderstanding, we need to be clear that this doesn't mean that we *stop* being human. On the contrary, we are most properly, most fully, human when we are able to live in this angelic liberty, because unless we grow into this, we are always going to be slipping down to being *less* than human. This, in fact, is one of the great messages that all the spiritual masters and mistresses have to share with us: if we're not growing, we're shrinking in the spiritual life. We can't just stand still. St Teresa of Ávila says, in describing the third level of the spirit's journey towards its centre, that either you go on or you go back – you can't simply stand still.[7] But, she says, there is a particular point in spiritual growth and discovery where the temptation will be just that – to stop, to think 'Oh, I think I've arrived at a settled spiritual life now, I'll just keep the wheels turning.' Beware, says Teresa firmly. If you think this, you are *already* slipping back. You always have to move beyond your spiritual comfort zone and keep growing. If you don't grow, you shrink, because you are measuring the journey by your own sense of satisfaction or achievement. Once you start saying, 'I must be about as human as I ought to be by now', you are treating your growing up in the spirit as a sort of possession, a definite and limited *thing*; and that is a sure route towards the diabolical, in which my individual needs and fancies are what set the standards for reality. But the authentically human life is one always extending out beyond itself towards the clarity and spaciousness of vision that God wants for us, towards an 'angelic' way of seeing the world that we are part of.

To set the scene, we shall rewind a little and reflect on what picture of the human heart itself is being taken for granted here. Appropriately, this takes us back to some radical first principles. There is God and there is creation (including ourselves). But why is there creation? God is self-sufficient, perfect, needing nothing in order just to be God. We can only imagine that there is what-is-not-God because God's abundant bliss is itself a sort of longing, a sort of internal pressure, we might almost say, for that joy to be shared. If this is right, then the only reason for creation is this internal pushing of the boundaries of God's love *by* God's love. The inner logic of divine love is that the divine life pours itself out to be lived by what isn't God in a movement of completely gratuitous gift. So the world comes into being at God's word, so that there will be a reflection and a sharing of the love that the Holy Trinity enjoys. And the love that the Holy Trinity enjoys, as St John's Gospel puts it in the Farewell Discourses of Jesus at the Last Supper, is about the beholding of *glory*. Remember Jesus' resonant words in that section of John's Gospel, the prayer that the disciples will share in 'the glory which I had with thee before the world was made' (Jn 17.5). Jesus prays to the Father for this sharing; it is what Jesus desires to share with us through the anguish of self-emptying which he is about to undergo, and it is what the resurrection delivers to us. So the rationale of your existence and mine is that 'glory' should be shared. We are made, unlikely though it sounds, for seeing and sharing glory.

Now, say the teachers of this tradition, it is this capacity/calling, the capacity of seeing and sharing the divine glory and joy, that is what is at the heart of our humanity. It is given various names: in Greek the most common is *nous* – a word sometimes translated as 'intellect', sometimes as 'mind'. But those words give a very misleading impression. The one thing *nous* is not is 'intellect' in our modern sense – the kind of intellectuality that gets you into university. Sobering as it may be for some of us, we have to recognize that the qualities that get you Oxbridge scholarships have little to do with what gets you into heaven ... Perhaps we should think of *nous* as the 'instinct' in us for seeing and loving what's real and what's true; a taste for the real, a kind of magnetic turning towards the real. And this means that *nous* is that capacity at the very centre of our being for turning Godwards, since God is what is unconditionally real. So when *nous* is identified, as it often is in Greek Christian literature, with the 'image of God' in us, this doesn't mean that God's image is in the mind rather than the body, or anything like that; it is simply saying that the centre of everything that we are as finite human subjects is this 'magnetic' turning in the direction of God – the iron filings twitching at the approach of the magnet, or perhaps the worm under the soil making its way towards the light, even though it doesn't know what's beyond the surface.

Nous, then, is the capacity for *contemplation*, the capacity for seeing, loving, absorbing, being transformed by what is supremely real – the life of God the Holy Trinity. This capacity is what makes us what we are. But here's the catch. This capacity grows and matures in us over time (that we live in time is simply part of being a limited and dependent being); it develops as we live a life involved with others, as we respond to situations and cope with a fluid and changing environment. The heart of what we are, this deep capacity and hunger in us for the real, can grow and develop only in such a context, because this is what it means for us to be created: God has made a changeable, interacting world, unlike the unchangeable divine self which is without beginning or end or transition. What is both wonderful and difficult is that God's unchangeable life is reflected in this changeable world, a world of diversity, interdependence, movement. God has so shaped the world that we grow into our deepest freedom in a world of constraints and challenges. There are implications here for thinking about the 'problem of evil' and ultimately about the rationale for creation itself, or about the nature of finite and infinite causation, but these need a different kind of book. They are all important in getting some sort of theoretical perspective on what it is to live in a world of limit and change, but our focus here is on the skills of living in a way that is faithful to what we most deeply are. We need to concentrate on the particular paradox that the brilliant, radiant capacity for growth and vision and sharing which is at the heart of our reality has to work itself out, to make itself fully real, in the middle of change and chance, which is where things begin to get complicated.

Change and chance confront us, and we respond. Around the centre within us of yearning and drawing towards the real there exists a whole system of response to our immediate material environment. We learn, both mentally and physically, to *react* to the situations that we're in; we learn the skills of survival in the world and we develop consistent strategies for finding our way through it by way of the images and concepts we construct as we move on. So there's a level of response in us that is to do with the instinctive coping with a world of change.

But it is this element of reactive response to the stimuli that come to us that is the level at which the most serious problems arise. We have to negotiate our way by means of these instincts, yet they can get in the way of our full humanity if we don't think through how they work. This level of our reality is what the monastic writers designate by the word 'passion', *pathos*. Yet again, we need some scare quotes or health warnings. What comes to mind when you hear the word 'passion'? Negatively speaking, perhaps sexual rapacity, furious anger? Positively speaking, deep commitment? (We're all expected in our CVs these days to say we have a 'passion' for whatever work we're applying for.) In the framework of the teaching we're looking at, all of this may well be part of the picture, but there is something more basic in view. For the Eastern Christian writers, 'passion' is the whole realm of instinct, reaction, coping mechanisms, and this is the level at which complications arise. We cannot live without these things if we are to be human at all; yet unless we understand and in some degree transfigure them, we are trapped in something less than human.[8]

It may be tempting to say (and some writers come uncomfortably close to saying it) that what you need to do is get rid of this entire level of human life, becoming a purely spiritual, purely free creature. But most of our sources in the literature say, in effect, good luck with that; but don't hold your breath. You're going to have to come to terms with 'passion'; you're going to have to learn to become spiritually *intelligent* about your instincts, to 'educate' your passions so as not to live at the level of reaction all the time. You are going to need to understand a bit of how these instinctual strategies work, where they help and where they hinder growth, where they stop you seeing clearly. If you can learn about this, you will know better how to cope when change and chance are battering you. Otherwise, you're going to be at the mercy of your instincts and passions, always *reacting*, never acting, stuck at the stage of responding to what you encounter just at the level of 'That looks nice' or 'That looks dangerous'. And going through life at that level is no recipe at all for a human existence that is intelligent or creative, a life growing as it reflects on itself and its interactions.

So what we are trying to bring into focus here is what is involved in being intelligent about the kind of beings we are and the kind of world we inhabit. And the classical sources point out that human beings from the start have made a spectacular train crash of this process. We have got so into the habit of being at the mercy of our instincts that we pass on from generation to generation the habits of imprisonment to unexamined instinct and self-defence. Our default setting as human beings has become a compound of anxiety, defensiveness and acquisitiveness; and this is why the monastic fathers can say (and there are already traces of this language in the New Testament) that the purpose of the life, death and resurrection of Jesus Christ, and the gift of his Holy Spirit, is the conquest of passion. It's a phrase that sounds odd to modern ears, but if we think of it in terms of the various blockages of our human freedom that our human habits have created – all that comes to be designated by the language about 'original sin', the spiritual handicaps we haven't chosen but are stuck with – we can perhaps see why our Christian forebears understood the heart of the Christian calling and the gift of Christ in these terms: why they regarded the life of freedom from passion – *apatheia* – as the resurrection life, the life of the Spirit in us.

There, then, is the big picture within which we are going to try and think about *apatheia* and the life of the passions. It is a picture in which the whole of the created universe is held and drawn together in God's purpose by the energy of this 'magnetic focusing' on God's own glory and beauty, the foundational reality in the finite world that reflects to God God's own giving, selfless, loving, contemplative reality. We cannot give precise content to all we say here, but we have come to think of divine life as somehow patterned as a mutual gaze of love and delight: the flow and return and overflow of divine life, what we speak of as the Father, the Son and the Spirit, is distinction without barriers, diversity without rivalry, neither plurality nor unity as we usually use those words. And that is our homeland, our *patria* in the language of the early Latin theologians like Augustine. This is where we belong; creation exists so that this bliss may be shared. If you think of the great icon of the Trinity by Andrei Rublev, you will recall that (as many commentators have noted) we who are looking into the icon are in effect occupying the vacant place on this side of the table around which the angelic figures representing the Trinity are placed; we are invited to grow into that place at the table. And all the literature about these things is simply about how we learn to unblock the path to get there.

From the fourth century onwards, Christians living in community, in and out of the desert, especially in Egypt and Syria, developed increasingly sophisticated diagnoses of how things could go wrong in our journey of liberation. This is how they began to formulate more detailed analyses of the 'passions of the soul' as we see them laid out by the great writers of those centuries. They wanted to do this diagnostic work so that they could understand themselves a bit better – not just for the sake of self-understanding but for the sake of liberation in love and communion, with God and with the rest of the world, human and non-human. They believed, of course, that this was only possible through the steady, continuing gift of the Holy Spirit, and they saw the process of coping with the passions as the process by which the baptismal gift could come alive in them. This is important to bear in mind: it's temptingly easy to think that this Eastern Christian literature is just a thinly cloaked description of general insights about 'mysticism' or about human liberation and self-realization, with little anchorage in the life of the Christian community and its sacraments or in the texts of the Bible. It helps to remember that they all see what they are exploring as grounded in the gift of baptism, and it's very revealing that they speak consistently of baptism as illumination. To be baptized is to be illuminated: 'Sleeper, awake! Rise from the dead, and Christ will shine on you', as we read in the Letter to the Ephesians (5.14), a passage that may well be taken from a very early Christian hymn. Christ will give you light; clarity of perception will be restored. You will no longer see the world either as a jungle or as a supermarket; you live with the promise of the risen life and the baptized vision, Christ's own vision of his divine Source laid open to you in the Spirit.

Not that this implies an utterly exclusive picture in which the Christian monastic teachers are defining a spiritual world completely alien to other models and idioms. They themselves naturally drew on the philosophy and psychology of their own world. They knew that the overall map of liberation from self-obsession and self-serving and the hope of a homecoming to the Unconditioned life from which all things derive shared common ground with many others. The difference was in the way they connected it with the embodied act of God in Jesus, and how his life and death and resurrection shaped the path by which healing could be found. In a modern context, they would have recognized that there was wisdom and even liberation to be found by listening to the experience of those who did not share the baptized identity, even if you held to the conviction that the entire shape of the process was marked out by Christ as the embodied Word or Mind of God.

In their own day they acknowledged that, quite a long way back in the tradition of philosophy beginning with Plato, you have the beginnings of a map of the inner life that starts to lay the foundations of something close to their own analyses. They recognized that Plato too thought that our destiny was to contemplate the truth; and, although in their eyes Plato did not have access to the full scope of that truth, he saw a vast amount of what needed to be seen, and offers the outline of a serviceable breakdown of the workings of the inner world. It is used by very diverse authors – even by Philo of Alexandria, the great Jewish commentator on the Torah in the first Christian century; by the time you get to the third century, Christian writers like Clement and Origen in the same lively and diverse intellectual culture of Alexandria are busy elaborating this kind of terminology further, and arguing with non-Christians who are exploring similar ideas.

So what does this incipient 'map' look like? As we have seen, there is in us a definitive or directive element, which is always – to use my earlier imagery – twitching towards a magnetic north, towards what is real. But then there are two bundles of instinct or reactive habit in us which are liable to destabilize this central element, even while performing tasks that are necessary for us. Plato famously used the image of a chariot drawn by two horses, with a charioteer struggling to keep it on track.[9] One of these bundles of instinct or habit is, very broadly speaking, something like aggression; the other, again very broadly speaking, something like desire. The first is what pushes things or people away, driven by a fear that the world is going to invade and violate or absorb us. The second is the opposite, which is the urge not to push away but to consume, to make what is there part of us, our needs, our agendas. Both exhibit a very problematic relation to reality. The first says, 'Go away, reality; I must keep myself safe and separate, and if you invade my territory I shall react with violence.' The second says, 'Come in here, reality; be absorbed in my narrative and my needs and I shall never have to think about you in your own terms.'

Two clusters of reactive habit: the Greeks seem to have associated these (in a way that is strikingly close to some of what you find in Buddhist anthropology and psychology) with different regions of the body. Being angry is, in Greek, literally being 'chesty': it is a gathering of energy in your chest, in the breast you might beat like a gorilla to demonstrate your strength and dominance; the Greek word is *thumos*. The impulse associated with desire and acquisition or consumption is *epithumia*, which belongs further down, in the lower belly. Part of what the Greeks, the Buddhists and the early Christians all agreed about was that what we had to do in our reflective or contemplative life was to get the *body* properly centred and balanced, with the assumption that disorder in either sphere affected the other, and the healing of one would likewise entail the healing of the other. But this basic threefold pattern – the foundational drawing to the real, plus the two bundles of reactive habit – is what is taken for granted in various ways throughout the Christian writings of the third century onwards; it persists in Greek writing on contemplation right to the end of the Middle Ages. The passions of aggression and desire are realities very much deeper than what we normally think of as just 'being angry' or 'being lustful or greedy': they cover all the mechanisms we use in responding to the world with either reactive and excluding fear, or with the urge to consume and absorb.

To be free from both of those is to find the balancing point of truthfulness where you can look at what is actually there in the world, and indeed in God, without either greed or defensive panic. This is why *apatheia* is connected – so surprisingly for the modern reader – with love.[10] Love is what happens when you stop being aggressive and greedy, and stop to look with your whole self, from the centre of who you are. It's as simple and as alarming as that. Love has room to flower when you stop either pushing reality away or making reality serve your purpose. In that space, love grows. God, remember, whose life is the ultimate definition of love, has neither aggression nor craving in the divine nature. God is not afraid, and God is not greedy. It sounds blindingly obvious, perhaps, put like that; but if we say that the love of God is, in the divine life, the same thing as the absence of aggression and greed, this ought to make us think that perhaps it tells us something of how love works – and fails to work – in us too. And if the work of Christ is to bring the love of God alive in our hearts, the implication is not too difficult to see.

So this is something of the 'big picture' I am attempting to work with. In these reflections I want to look further at how these instincts and passions are broken down and analysed by the great writers of the early monastic world. But I also want to make a rather ambitious suggestion about how to think about the *positive* side of this, about what the free life looks like; and this is to propose that you can read the analysis of the 'passions of the soul' in the monastic writers alongside the Beatitudes which Jesus utters in St Matthew's Gospel. The monastic theologians identify altogether eight passions of the soul; and it so happens that there are eight Beatitudes. And it is possible to see the Beatitudes as a series of 'crystallizations' of what it might be to live a life free of the corresponding eight distortions or passions. A tool for reflection. I may or may not be right in trying to link these together. Over to the reader.

But to conclude this introductory sketch, what may be helpful is to hold in mind the most basic truth of all: we are, because God is. And we are *what we* are because God is *what God* is. God is eternally, necessarily, unchangingly, the infinity of love and exchange, mutuality. What God does in making the world is rooted in the overflowing of that mutuality, that sharing of bliss. The only rationale for creation is so that love can be shared. God did not make creation out of boredom or loneliness, finding an outlet for frustrated creativity, as we might say. God made the world gratuitously, so that there would be love in what was not God.

And this means that what is really most significant about us as creatures, finite beings who have been brought into existence, is what I have called the 'worm under the soil', the 'magnetic quivering', the capacity to share and reflect, to *contemplate* – which is a good deal more than just sitting and gazing. It is absorbing life, being drawn into life, communicating life. It's in this light that we are to understand the various distortions and pitfalls surrounding this path. These distortions and pitfalls are rooted in something perfectly natural to us – the life of instinct; and yet, because we humans are, alas, quite ingenious beings, they can be distorted in all sorts of ways to serve our unexamined and unreflecting egos; so that instead of just being basically survival mechanisms to secure some basic stability, they become something much more sinister – a way of 'de-realizing' and dissolving the reality in front of us. And so they become the traps and chains from which we need deliverance.

Christ is incarnate, lives, dies, rises from the dead, breathes out the Holy Spirit so that those chains will be broken – so that we are able to become human in quite a new way, human in a way that allows what Evagrius calls the 'angelic' to be alive in us – the wondering perception of what is. It is a vision not from some perspective floating far above the earth but from the perspective of embodied living – yet 'angelic' in clarity, in truthfulness and in the freedom and compassion that come from this.

PART ONE

PART ONE

I

MAPPING THE PASSIONS
OF THE SOUL

We shall start in this chapter with a few introductory comments on the broad framework within which the monastic tradition understands these issues, and then move on to the detail of what is said about specific passions and instincts – and into a consideration of the Beatitudes of Jesus as a set of 'counter-proposals', modes of living that develop as responses to 'passion'. But first it may help to look briefly at how the early monastic writers approach the question of *temptation* – the unsettlement of the mind which can release the exercise of passion. This is an important topic, if only because there remains a fair level of confusion about the subject of temptation in some modern Christian thinking. If we lack some of the tools that the tradition offers for understanding this, we shall miss some significant insights into the different levels at which will and imagination are engaged in this process of being 'tempted'.[1]

The Greek word itself, *peirasmos*, simply means 'testing' (it has connections with 'empirical' study – study that can be tested – and the idea of experiment, putting something to the proof). There are various levels of test, as (literally and unhappily) every school student knows, and one of the helpful and pastorally sensitive dimensions of the early Eastern tradition is to distinguish very clearly between those levels. It's important, say the texts of this period, to be honest about what is actually going on in us; registering that we feel some kind of impulse, some kind of drawing to a particular activity or response, is part of what we must look at and deal with responsibly. There is no point in sitting on it, denying it, running away from it or simply trying not to think of it because, as we all know, trying *not* to think of something is a fool's errand (as if someone were to say to us, 'Don't, whatever you do, think of the word "hippopotamus" for the next five minutes ...').

At first, then, we simply 'register'; we note that, yes, this is happening to me, there is an impulse (what the Greek calls a 'prompt' or 'prod', *probole*) which, given time and circumstance, could develop. But then the slippery slope begins. There is the first flicker, which we could paraphrase roughly as 'That's interesting'

4

(rather than just registering that it's happening) and perhaps 'That's welcome'. There is thus, say the texts, an initial 'interruption' of the mind's working, and then (translating the Greek word literally) a 'pairing off' with it. I might even think, 'What a complicated and interesting person I must be to have these impulses'. I begin to explore the impulse a little, to turn it over in my mind, to give it house room. And the next stage is to begin to see it positively, to treat it as something worth exploring or imagining in detail. My mind sets to work on it: 'I could do this, I might enjoy that.' Before you know where you are, you are *consenting* to it – that is, you are not only welcoming it, you are, so to speak, putting a meal on the table for it and getting it a bed for the night. You are deliberately giving it a place in your mind or heart and agreeing to be led by it. This leads to a 'laying hold of' what's there and a connecting of it with memories of past experience and action, and the final outcome is the loss of freedom – the passive state of what we might call addiction.

This is a condensation of quite a long bit of discussion in the work of a writer called Hesychios,[2] who lived perhaps in the ninth century, a discussion that is seriously helpful in pastoral and personal terms because it tells us two crucial things: first, that it's important to be honest about what's in our minds, and second, that we need to be very aware of the ways in which we can slip from that honesty into a rather corrupting *fascination* with ourselves. We are all rather liable to find ourselves interesting in this lightly novelistic way, and it is a major problem to overcome if we are to be free. The notion – which is surely fundamental to the gospel – that, whether or not we're 'interesting', we're *lovable* from God's point of view is often hard to grasp. Most of us rather relish the idea that we are or could be dramatic, unusual, complicated and are easily persuaded to play around with the drama.

So as to resist the temptation of simply burrowing around in our insides – as opposed to the honest registering of what is actually going on in us – we need to learn some skills in discernment. It involves walking a bit of a knife-edge between obsessive self-analysis and bland unawareness (and frequently getting it wrong, no doubt). What the desert writers are trying to underline for us is, fundamentally, two things. One is (as so often in the writings of this period) a sort of 'Don't panic' message: be aware of impulses or inclinations, but don't be obsessively anxious. There it is; face it. And then, the second thing: give it to God. Don't flatter it with lots of (satisfying) exploration, fantasy and drama. Give it to God; and then go and do the washing up, or dig the garden, or take out the rubbish; go and visit a sick friend or say your prayers. Register what's there, then take the next step of your life.

When we read in Evagrius or Cassian or any of the other great teachers of the monastic tradition about the analysis of the 'passions of the soul' and how they affect us, we are learning something of the background these teachers want to be able to assume in their day-to-day work of formation in the monastic communities – and indeed in Christian communities more widely. It is not surprising, then, that one of the basic notions developed in this environment is a way of thinking about these pressures to pursue and obsess about the passions. The desert teachers discuss the power of what we could call corrupt chains of thought – *logismoi* in Greek; literally just 'thoughts', but used to signify the kind of 'fugue' of obsession that makes us prisoners of destructive patterns within us. We're constantly being told to avoid *logismoi,* being caught up in obsessive patterns. If we are 'enslaved' by passion, it is because the chains we forge for ourselves are, as often as not, just habits of this kind, the fruit of anxiety and fantasy. This can be fantasy of all sorts: the fantasies we have about 'what I should have said to her at that moment so as to get my own back or get on top of the situation' or 'what I should have done in that event where I made that disastrously wrong call' or 'how glad I am about that event where I think I got it right and how

much I want others to know about it' … and all the
rest, all that world in which I am the centre of what
matters, and need all the time to be proved right and
good. This is what is meant by *logismoi,* just as much
as the equally familiar series of fantasies that bedevil
our sexual imagining – the things that so many people
seem to think of as the only serious kind of temptation.
They are all equally *chains* of thought, not just strings
of connected mental rambling but chains that bind us,
different kinds of trap.

The analysis of the different levels or stages of
temptation is designed to stop us stepping into these
traps and getting stuck – so that, instead, we can
recognize, acknowledge before God, give into the hands
of God and pass on. And clarifying this is something
with which we need one another's help: we must get
used to talking things through with an experienced
guide at some length – not quite as if we were in therapy
or analysis but just to learn how to see ourselves with
some detachment. If you expose your 'thoughts', your
logismoi, to a spiritual father or mother, this both
keeps you humble about the tangles you live with and
offers some saving clarity about what matters most,
so that it is very different from the fascinating private
world where I continuously star as the hero or heroine
of my own little dramas, with applauding multitudes,
and from the equally dangerous private world in

which I pick over my failures with disgust. Finding this way forward is easier said than done, but this is what the great teachers are after: honesty without self-indulgence, a ballet dancer's point of pivot and balance. Very hard to get right, so don't be surprised if you go on getting it wrong; but once again, learn to be aware without panic that this is what's happening.

One other preliminary point is simply to introduce the most extensive tool of diagnosis in the tradition – the actual catalogue of the passions. I mentioned before that for most early writers in the Greek tradition there are two basic clumps of instinct – the aggressive and the greedy. Evagrius at the end of the fourth century elaborates this in terms of three primary 'groups of demons' who assault those setting out on the ascetical life, demons who specialize in gluttony, avarice and self-esteem.[3] He breaks this down further into *eight* basic habits or conditions of the soul.[4] It is the origin of our language in the West about the 'seven deadly sins', a somewhat simplified account of the earlier analysis; and to call them 'sins' is not quite what the early tradition means. What had been a helpful pastoral tool of analysis turned into something more like a list of 'kinds of wrong action'; and in that process some of the force and clarity of the earlier analysis was lost. Some of us who had an impeccable Anglo-Catholic upbringing will have learned the list of the seven deadly sins in confirmation class, perhaps with a little mnemonic to remember them: PLAGUES – pride, lust, anger, gluttony, usury, envy, sloth. Not without its uses, not at all a bad peg on which to hang some self-examination before confession. But there is a significant difference of emphasis between a list of wrong actions and a diagnosis of how our impulses, not necessarily evil in themselves, just a way of coping in a complicated world, can become destructive and compulsive in their effects.

The order in which they are listed sometimes varies, but Evagrius and a little later Cassian (early in the fifth century) offer what becomes a classic order, moving from straightforward physical longings to pride as the summation of all that is wrong in us.[5] We begin with *greed* or *gluttony*, learning to control the impulse to satisfy not just basic hunger. The longing to feel full and satisfied is the key to all other sorts of physical self-restraint, so that dealing with this is essential to managing the next problem, the prompting of sexual fantasy and rapacity, the passion of *lust*. Greed directed towards things and greed towards persons are closely linked; and this is reinforced by the fact that *avarice* comes next in the list. Cassian distinguishes it from greed and lust because those are essentially the misuse of natural internal impulses not in themselves blameworthy, while avarice is prompted from outside and is manifest in possessiveness and fear about the future: 'Will I be safe, will I be able to protect myself?' And this leads to a kind of idolatry, where the dread of insecurity infects everything and provokes resentment and misery. *Anger* comes next, treated primarily as something that 'blinds the eyes of the heart' and makes discernment impossible. Cassian describes how he himself has experienced anger against inanimate objects in his manual work, and insists on patience as the remedy, along with the constant monitoring of our reaction to others so as to root out resentment. The next on the list is *dejection*, which is also connected with the loss of our capacity to see clearly: we lose sight of what we are capable of; we lower our sights and expect the worst of ourselves. In contrast to real sorrow for sin, which looks to renewal and transformation, dejection traps us in the past, in negative pictures of who we are. It is close to, but not identical with, *listlessness* – *acedia* in Greek – which is a kind of self-indulgent lassitude ('Whatever'), a state of mind both restless and torpid, an inability to settle to anything and a vague feeling of discontent. Monks are especially vulnerable to this in the eyes of Evagrius and Cassian, living as they do in a confined context with what can feel a drab and repetitive pattern in daily life. It is a condition in which just doing the next thing that needs doing becomes harder and harder. Finally, we come to *self-esteem* and *pride* – once again, close but different. Self-esteem is a plain matter of ambition for status and reputation, and Cassian describes how adaptable it can be; if we can't persuade ourselves that we are admirable for one reason, we shall rapidly think of another. But pride is 'fiercer than all that have been discussed up till now', a complete surrender to illusion in that it involves a refusal to acknowledge the gift of God as the foundation for all that we are and do: it is effectively to treat oneself as God, and thus is the most comprehensive state of falsehood imaginable.

This sketch of how the eight passions are understood may help to make it clear why we are talking here not simply about wrong acts but about ways in which natural impulses can be distorted and can cloud our perception. Reactions of repulsion can be useful when we are faced with genuinely anti-human pressures and temptations. There is nothing wrong with hunger and the desire to eat, or even with sexual desire in itself. But when these impulses are experienced and thought about independently of their context and purpose, they breed a steadily growing family of habits that make truthful perception impossible, ending in the lethal delusion that we are what we are independently of God's radical and free gift of existence. And in this light, sin is the ultimate form of misunderstanding and revolt against what is truly natural to us, a repudiation of what at some level we know to be for our health and well-being. A 'sinful' individual is indeed held responsible for their consent to such delusive myths (remember our earlier discussion of the different stages of temptation). But the fact that we are able to give this consent, and that we do it so readily, arises from a deeper problem, the problem analysed by St Paul in the Letter to the Romans, as he probes that level of our identity in which we inherit, or are born into, an entire human environment in which, bizarrely and mysteriously, saying no to God feels easier than saying yes. It is indeed a bizarre state of affairs because, given what we are actually made for, it takes quite a bit of human ingenuity and quite a lot of practice across human history to get us to this extraordinary point: as if over the centuries we had trained ourselves to write holding the pen between our little finger and thumb. It's quite an art; it takes practice to become used to something so illogically wrong. But that is what the heritage of sin means.

This is why the teachers of the early monastic era, and some of the great figures of slightly later generations who write up their legacy, are both ultra-serious about sin and deeply compassionate about it. They have no illusion whatever about the destructive consequences of sin; sooner or later, if you insist on writing with your little finger and thumb, things are going to go wrong with your hand. Sin costs us; it costs us our human *naturalness*; it freezes up our liberty to say yes to what we are most deeply, naturally, oriented to. A huge price to pay for our mistakes and confusions; and yet these teachers recognize that in pretty well every context where we give way, where we let ourselves be pushed around, manipulated, bullied, you might say, by forces around us, it is no help to pretend that it is all just a matter of our own individual fault. We are deeply vulnerable, and there are considerable powers at work against us.

These are the powers that the monastic teachers call 'demons'. We're encouraged in this literature to take them seriously – but not too seriously. In our inherited muddle and delusion, as we go on pretending that we are somehow independent of our creator, we are very much at the mercy of forces around us which are also at odds with their deepest reality. Forget the mythical apparatus of horns and tails: demons are simply non-human energies that are cut loose from their moorings in the truth and are all too ready to reinforce and nurture our own unreality. When Evagrius writes about this,[6] he talks about how the attacks of the demons are really forces that are, as it were, exploiting and nagging away at what is already in our imaginations. They don't necessarily have to appear in dramatic external forms. They are simply those forces that feed themselves into our minds and hearts when we are weak and confused, when we are already not at home with ourselves, when our sense of who we are is cramped by the habit of twisting ourselves into bizarre postures and so on; then the diabolical, the contrarian and deceitful forces, those whatever-they-are that are at odds with God and good in the universe, find a foothold, the drip-feed of delusion is strengthened, and more and more fantasy is generated.

Like temptation, demons need to be acknowledged, but they definitely do *not* need to be the focus of excessive interest. As soon as you show interest in them – just as when you show interest in yourself and your fascinatingly complicated insides – you actually open the door more widely. So anything like advanced degrees in demonology, a fascination with the diabolical, is exactly the wrong way to deal with this. It's been said that the desert fathers approach the diabolical both with a sense of awe and with something approaching mischief. The diabolical forces are indeed out to get you, but their fundamental refusal of reality means that they are both cunning and not very bright. The sensible and realistic Christianized intelligence will be able to outwit them. There are stories of desert fathers encountering frustrated demons wandering around in the wilderness kicking the stones, so to speak, and grumbling that they cannot get anywhere near the great monks because these 'great old men/women' already know that they are sinners; the demons, who are always trying desperately both to make them sin and to make them despair over their sin, are frustrated because the holy elders will respond to their effort by saying, 'Of course I'm a sinner. So what? I rely only on the mercy of God.' It is this kind of humility that most effectively frustrates the demons.

In the long run, the pattern of integrated, restored human life that we're called to and drawn to in the labour of prayer and service and love is in all sorts of ways – quite appropriately – a prosaic matter, a matter of *doing the next thing*. If you're worried about temptation, go on saying the Psalms and doing your manual work and checking your thoughts for grievance, resentment and self-regard. When Cassian writes about the self-denial appropriate for combating the passion of greed and lust, he notes that you can make life infinitely more difficult for yourself by overdoing the asceticism, just as you can overdo the indulgence.[7] Don't be preoccupied with what a great model of self-denial you are becoming; concentrate on the question 'What has God asked me to just get on with?'

It is this prosaic quality that makes so much of this literature appealing and practical. At times, as any reader of the literature will know, we encounter a vocabulary and a set of assumptions about the kind of life you are leading which is a bit off-putting; the routine severities of the monastic life in the eastern Mediterranean in the fifth century or thereabouts are not where we are starting today, and they seem alien and exotic to us. But pierce through this surface level, and you see the common sense, the realism and, above all, the fundamental level of trust in God that is required in all this. This trust in God is trust in a God who sees us with exactly the clarity we hope and pray for and doesn't turn away. And so, when we learn discernment or discrimination, when we learn to see ourselves properly and pick apart some of the positive and the negative impulses as they work themselves out in us, we come to reflect something of God's own freedom from 'passion', God's own *apatheia* towards us. God does not see us reactively; God is not roused to fury and disgust by the sight of us – nor is God persuaded to love us because we are so successful. God sees what is there, embraces it in His love and transforms it in His grace – the essence of the Gospel of Jesus Christ. If we start being frightened or disgusted by ourselves, something is going amiss; we are not loving ourselves as God loves us.

This is not a bland New-Age-ish message of self-acceptance – because God does actually want to make a difference. God embraces and loves us as we are, but the presence of God in the neighbourhood of ourselves cannot but affect what we are: we can't live in the proximity of truth and be comfortable with lies. God's purpose is our life, and we cannot live in unreality. Back to the recognition that sin costs. God knows the cost of sin better than any of us can imagine. 'There was no other good enough to pay the price of sin,' we sing on Good Friday; and this brilliantly simple distillation of the atonement tells us what we need to know – that God has carried the cost of a sinful world, has taken on and absorbed all the consequence of rebellion and refusal, right to the end. God knows the cost and does not look away.

Before moving on from this preliminary sketch of the diagnosis and analysis of passion we might revisit something touched on earlier, which is the importance of seeing the whole vision of the life of freedom, discernment, clarity, liberty from enslaved and enslaving instinct and so on as the *manifestation of the Holy Spirit* – not simply some human ideal. A couple of passages from the *Philokalia* bring this into focus: here, once again, is the great Diadochos (and remember that the English word 'intellect' is not a very adequate translation of the Greek *nous*, which includes far more of what we would think of as intuition and contemplation):

It is clear that the intellect [*nous*] cannot be the common dwelling place of God and the devil. How can St Paul say that 'with my intellect I serve the law of God, but with the flesh the law of sin' (Rom. 7.25), unless the intellect is completely free to engage in battle with the demons, gladly submitting itself to grace? He can only say this because the wicked spirits of deception are free to lurk in the bodies of those pursuing a spiritual way; 'for I know that in me – that is, in my flesh – there dwells nothing good' (Rom. 7.18), says the Apostle. Here he is not merely expressing a personal opinion. The demons attack the intellect, but they do so by trying through lascivious temptations to entice the flesh down the slope of sensual pleasure. It is for a good purpose that the demons are allowed to dwell within the body even of those who are struggling vigorously against sin; for in this way man's free will is constantly put to the test. If a man, while still alive, can undergo death through his labours, then in his entirety he becomes the dwelling place of the Holy Spirit; for such a man, before he has died, has already risen from the dead, as was the case with the blessed Apostle Paul, and all those who have struggled and are struggling to the utmost against sin.[8]

In other words, what we are really talking about is the resurrection life, the life of a humanity that has become the dwelling place of the Holy Spirit, the life that is realized when we learn to understand and live with and through all the temptations and impulses that might swamp our small boats. 'For we groan, earnestly desiring to be clothed with our house that is from heaven ... so that what is mortal in us may be swallowed up by life': St John the Carpathian (possibly writing in the seventh century) quotes these words from 2 Corinthians 5.4, and continues: 'not only in the case of the body after the consummation of this age, but also by anticipation here and now, spiritually. For "death is swallowed up in victory" (1 Cor. 15.54); all the pursuing Egyptians that harass us will be swallowed up in the waves, when power is sent down upon us from heaven'.[9] It is our exodus we are talking about, our passage through the Red Sea, our movement into the land of difficult but eventually transforming freedom.

This imagery, so prominent in the Easter liturgy – of passing through the Red Sea, escaping slavery, travelling ultimately into the promised land but by a long and circuitous route with much experience of directionless darkness – was of the greatest importance to writers of the early Christian period. We have been saved from captivity, liberated from those forces, internal and external, that destabilize and dehumanize us. We have been confronted by a mystery of love, so overwhelming, so indescribable, that it can be terrifying – so much so that, like the Israelites wandering around the Sinai Peninsula in the biblical story, we sometimes think that it would be easier to go back. But remember what we noted earlier about the temptation to go back: the truth is that we cannot stay still. We grow or we shrink. But ultimately, if we can find our way through the disorientation, the fear about the future, there is milk and honey at the end of the journey (the milk and honey that in the early baptismal rites were given to the newly baptized); there is resurrection here and now, the Holy Spirit coming to be at home in human lives. If that is what we want, and if our wanting is placed into the hands of the risen Christ who intercedes for us, we are able to trust God to bring us home.

2

PRIDE, LISTLESSNESS AND THE
TRUTH OF DEPENDENCE

Time now to look at the passions of the soul in turn, as they are analysed and understood by the monastic tradition we have been exploring; and I want to suggest a link between these passions and the gospel Beatitudes, seeing the eight Beatitudes of St Matthew's Gospel as a sort of reversed image of the things that go wrong in our souls.

As we have noted, most analyses of the passions and the destructive impulses of the soul take pride as the root of everything that goes wrong – which is why pride often comes either at the beginning or at the end of the lists. Cassian comes to it last of all: it is 'a most fierce demon', he says, more sinister than anything he has discussed so far. And Cassian notes that, whereas the other passions and instincts of the soul nibble away at bits of our selfhood, pride strikes at the very root, destroys it completely, razing it to its foundations. 'The angel who fell from heaven because of his pride bears witness to this. He had been created by God and endued with every virtue and all wisdom, but he did not want to ascribe this to the grace of the Lord. He ascribed it to his own nature.'[1]

In other words, pride is at heart a failure to accept *dependence* gratefully and gracefully, a failure to accept our dependence. 'Oh, but,' we say, 'aren't we meant to be independent? Isn't autonomy, adult responsibility the great thing that we ought all to be working for?' To this, the Christian gospel says both yes and no. There is a completely proper kind of self-determination; freedom is part of how we activate the image of God in us. But – and it is a pretty substantial 'but' – we are, like it or not, dependent, minute by minute, on all we have received and are receiving. We are dependent for our humanity on our parentage, our upbringing; we're dependent for our life, moment by moment, on our breathing and our eating. As persons we are constantly receiving, absorbing; and if we try to deny that, once again we become not more but less human. And, in the life of the Spirit, and our life in relation to God, recognizing this is crucial.

Remember the phrase used earlier: we are because God is. We are the way we are because of the way God is, and so to be fully ourselves is to grow into an awareness of God. Without this we would not be. It's as basic a rule as taking the next breath. And just as we were thinking earlier about sin as a kind of ultra-complicated distortion of our humanity, like trying to write with the thumb and the little finger, so pride, we could say, is trying to hold your breath until you burst, like very small children in a fit of temper.

Pride is the refusal to breathe in and let God be what God is – which is the heart and focus of energy of our being. So when Cassian talks about the first angel who fell as illustrating the perils of self-reliance, that's what he has in mind. The angel who fell, the archangel Lucifer, looks at God and says, 'God is great and beautiful and wonderful – and therefore a rival. I am great and beautiful and wonderful, and I want to be greater, more wonderful, more beautiful than God.' But when you see God as a rival – out there threatening you just by being God – what you don't see is that God cannot be a rival: God is *already* your life, and there's nothing you can do about it. God is always, already your life.

You are because God is; forget that, and you condemn yourself to a sort of shadow existence. Various people have said about the fallen archangel that he's ingenious but very stupid. It's important to remember sometimes that the Devil, the energy of destructiveness, is (like all the demons, as we saw earlier) vastly cunning and resourceful, but very

24

stupid at root. I'm sure you've sometimes seen a cat stalking a bird, the cat looking very cunning and moving very carefully and stealthily while the bird sits on the branch watching it; and at the crucial moment it simply flies away as the cat pounces. Sometimes to see the Prince of Darkness as a rather dim cat stalking a bird, with a great apparatus of cunning and resourcefulness but a fundamental failure to see what's going on, may be helpful in keeping the Devil in his place.

So the right kind of dependence – knowing we are because God is, knowing that the root of our very being is the self-giving of God – is what we have to learn. This is where the connection with the first of the Beatitudes arises. 'Blessed are the poor in spirit,' say the traditional translations. The New English Bible famously rendered this as 'Happy are those who know their need of God' – not at all a bad rendering, in fact, because 'the poor' in the Hebrew Scriptures are not simply the economically poor. When the Psalms talk about 'the congregation of the poor', they are referring to God's people as a whole – a community fully aware that they can't be anything, or do anything or have anything without God. The congregation of the poor, in other words, are those who are aware they are because God is. So when Jesus uses that phrase, 'the poor in spirit', it is not difficult to imagine that this background is what is coming through, the tradition in the Hebrew world of thinking of God's people as those who acknowledge that their identity is grounded in God.

So the poor in 'spirit' (*pneuma* in Greek) are those who are aware of their own *pneuma,* their breathing in and out, as that which carries the sense of their dependence. They know that their own breathing in and out happens only within and because of the deep flowing in and flowing out of God in them, the life-giving breath that is God's gift. It is significant that the word for 'spirit' is the word for 'breath' – so that when we speak of 'the life of the Spirit', it is like imagining an extra dimension of our breathing, some further depth in our lungs and belly that allows us to be filled more profoundly. The 'blessedness' of those who know that they are because God is, is the blessedness of those who know that, within, beneath and beyond their breathing in and out is the very breath of God, the life-giving Spirit breathed on the infant church by the risen Jesus (Jn 20.20).

How do we learn to deal with pride, then? Not by artificially putting ourselves down but by putting ourselves 'in', into the rhythm of God's breath; not by pretending we are less than we truly are but by knowing where our roots are; by recognizing that God is not a rival facing off with us but the depth within that seeks constantly to let life arise more fully in us. The answer to pride is 'poverty of spirit' – recognizing your need of God.

And then Jesus in St Matthew's text goes on immediately to speak of the blessedness of 'mourning', the blessedness of those who are sorrowful, promising them consolation. Can we imagine that the blessedness of those who mourn can be seen as a contrast to, and remedy for, what the writers of the monastic tradition call *acedia* – listlessness, indifferent shrugging of the shoulders? Those who mourn, those who are sorrowful, are those who *care,* those who are capable of feeling loss for what it is.

When we look at the analysis of listlessness and apathy in the monastic literature, what we see described is both boredom and the wrong kind of detachment, both a sort of exhaustion and a shrugging off of things, a hardening of the heart. It's analysed with great skill in some of the early texts: Evagrius has a fine passage on why this passion is called the 'noon-day demon', imagining the solitary in the desert as the sun rises higher in the sky and there's nothing really to do until bedtime except weave baskets and say Psalms.[2] Frankly, it's proving pretty unrewarding, and the monk says to himself, 'I could be so much more useful, I could be leading such a fruitful life. I'm sure someone needs to hear from me. I know – I'll visit a neighbour and give them good advice. I have so much to give, I'm wasted in this solitude.' A steady expansion of the ego and its fantasies becomes a way of concealing from yourself the poverty that you have to live with. You're trying to fill the void with fantasies about who you might be, and, because you're just trying to fill the void, you are avoiding the underlying poverty, and the basic necessity of just 'parking' the ego and its business. This is why indulging the noonday demon will eventually produce more lassitude not less, more self-disgust and impatience and resentment.

Acedia, listlessness, the awareness of a dreariness in one's life; all of this leads, ultimately, either to a breakdown or to a breakthrough. The 'breakdown' may not be very visible; it may be just a matter of growing a surface layer of cynicism, non-commitment, coping habits that get you through the next 24 hours. Underneath the 'Whatever' attitude is a habit of protecting yourself steadily more from the real cost of living with dependence, with poverty and with the uncertainty and, yes, the boredom that goes with it.

I'm sure I am not the only bishop who has preached at confirmations along the line that the candidates will have to get used to dull and unrewarding phases of Christian life: the last thing you may want to hear at a celebratory event, especially as a young believer or a new convert. But the truth is that ordinary grown-up human life is sometimes dull. Accept it, embrace it, live through it and the familiar advice: don't panic. If you try and conquer boredom by fantasy, by building up satisfying pictures of yourself, by nostalgia, resentment, wistfulness for the person you might have been, all the things that might feel helpful in combating boredom, you will ultimately be choosing fiction over truth.

But listen to that strange blessing for those who mourn. Don't be afraid of acknowledging that this *hurts*; don't be afraid of acknowledging that the world itself hurts. The worst thing that can happen to you is a kind of anaesthesia of the spirit – somehow not noticing your own hurt or the hurt of others. It doesn't mean that you will be submerged in that hurt. You will only learn not to be trapped in suffering when you acknowledge its reality and look for its sources.

St Mark the Ascetic – another of the great figures of the early centuries – says:

The remembrance of God is suffering of heart endured in a spirit of devotion. If you forget God, you become self-indulgent and insensitive [in the Greek, *anaisthetos* – anaesthetized]. Do not say

that a person free from passion cannot suffer
affliction. Even if he does not suffer on his own
account he's liable to do for his neighbour.

Being free from passion does not mean being free
from pain and suffering. Difficult, yet again, to find
the balance: not that one invites suffering or wallows
in it, but that one acknowledges one's own pain and
grief honestly, and acknowledges the grief of the
neighbour honestly; that one carries in compassion
the need of the neighbour as one's own. Mourning,
sorrowing, is part of the life of freedom. What a
very strange thing that sounds, but think of the
opposite: a life in which we constantly blocked off
mourning, denied our own suffering and sat light to
the suffering of others. That would be a deeply unreal
and dishonest life, pretending to be what we're not,
pretending that the world is what it is not; not a good
recipe for freedom, which always requires a keen
sense of what the real constraints are.

So the opposite of listlessness – the opposite of all
those restless coping mechanisms, those various ways
of wriggling out of boredom and frustrated self-
esteem, shifting our gaze away from pain in myself
or the world – is the freedom to mourn, the freedom
to say to God, 'I acknowledge my pain, my sense of
loss, and I'm not hiding from it. I acknowledge that

the world is scarred with injustice and suffering, and I bring it to you, knowing that I'm here to speak it aloud in your presence.' It is why the great protests and laments of the Psalms have always been so deeply embedded in the prayers of Jews and Christians. It is why St Augustine can say that we need to remember constantly that it is Christ who prays the Psalms with us and in us; it is Christ who is mourning and lamenting on behalf of the world before God in the Psalms, and we as the body of Christ share his lament over sin and injustice because the world's evils are our own loss, each one of us, not another's.

Christ suffers for the world. Christ suffers once and for all. Christ presents the pain of the world before God in the heavenly sanctuary. Yes, but also we as Christ's body catch the echoes of that eternal lament and that eternal intercession and, as Christ has made it his own, we make our prayer and our protest his own. We mourn with him; we lament for our sin and the sin and grief of the world, and we express in that mourning our trust in Christ's freedom to be alongside all suffering and to transfigure the damaged world.

Jesus begins the Beatitudes by pointing us to poverty of spirit – our capacity to recognize our dependence – and then urges us to acknowledge the pain and suffering which we share with the family of all creatures on earth. So, in looking at these first pairings of passion and beatitude, we can begin to grasp how the first two ways in which Jesus points to the life of the Kingdom, poverty of spirit and freedom for lament, guide us in seeing how we are turned away from pride and apathy, turned from the refusal to admit dependence and the refusal to admit vulnerability. There the seeds are sown for our further growth into what we might be and what God wants us to be – towards that clarity of vision and of love which is God's purpose for our humanity.

3

ANGER, GLUTTONY AND THE GRACE
OF POVERTY

One of the most interesting features of the literature we have been looking at is that many of these writers have what you might call a soft spot for anger. Anger is a passion about which there are some good things to say, because the aggressive (what the standard *Philokalia* translation calls the 'incensive') power has more in the way of positive uses than some other elements of the internal menagerie. You can helpfully turn your anger against certain things.[1] Yet this is also one of the aspects of anger that make it dangerous. We all know that 'righteous anger' is commendable in some circumstances; we all know how powerfully seductive it can be, what a successful alibi it is for self-justification. Anger is properly used, say the early texts, against our own laziness, untruthfulness and corruption. It is properly directed against injustice and suffering that could be changed in the world around us. Anger, indeed, is given to us as a passion so that we may have an energetic and transforming response to the failures of ourselves and our world; it stops us being resigned, being passive in the face of the fact that we are not what we are called to be and are capable of being.

So far, so good. But think about the language we sometimes hear, of anger as a 'red mist before the eyes', or a ringing in the ear, as a physical pulsation and disturbance. The monastic writers would have recognized this; and one of the important things they have to say about it is that, no matter what provokes it, even when it is aimed at an evil that ought to be combated, anger has a blinding effect. Cassian notes that 'anger dwells in the heart and blinds the eyes of the heart with sombre disorders'. He uses a vivid image about this universal ambivalence about anger: whether a leaf is made of gold or lead, if it's lying on top of your eye you still can't see. The 'gold' of righteous, transforming anger and the 'lead' of self-serving, sullen, resentful anger have the same effect of limiting what you can see. This is why discernment is particularly important here: even the most 'righteous' anger must be looked at and thought about, so that it does not become something indulged, enjoyed. There is such a thing as righteous or appropriate anger, but it will slip readily into self-righteous anger, a passionate habit that serves our illusions about ourselves.

One of the best summaries of this is a phrase from a book by a missionary deeply involved in work with the deprived and abused poor in rural African communities.[2] He imagines himself in prayer being confronted by the question 'Whom does your anger serve?' In other words, are these feelings of indignation and protest about making you feel better, or are they about the energy to change things? It's a question worth repeating because it so clearly crystallizes the dangers. Anger that primarily serves me, the release of my emotions, the conviction of my rightness, the illusion of my control and power, is a risky business, threatening to make me less able to see what (inside and outside) needs to change.

The proper use, the proper understanding of anger, according to Cassian and others, is that it is something that has to be focused on our own malicious and destructive thoughts, and on the destructiveness around us. It has a proper use, and in this literature it is often the cardinal example of how the 'passions of the soul' are natural instincts that should not be simply denied or repressed, but which do, emphatically and urgently, need to be named and understood in terms of their proper purpose. If we do not know what is going on with our anger, then the leaves are plastered over our eyes; the cause of it, good or bad, is irrelevant. We can lethally damage our souls by righteous anger as much as unrighteous, in the long run, if the effect of such anger is simply the blinding that Cassian describes.

This brings us back to the fundamental point in all our struggles to understand and cope with the passions. What we most need is *realism* – a realism about the kind of beings we are, beings who grow in the love and service of God, in the very image of God, within the context of a world of movement and uncertainty in which we are not in charge. This is why the natural partner for anger, among the Matthaean Beatitudes, is the third in the list: 'Blessed are the meek.' And yet again we are faced with a problem of vocabulary. 'Meek' is not a word that is easy to salvage; even 'humble', which is sometimes used as an alternative in translations, is not a great deal better. The immediate associations are with the embarrassing self-deprecation of Dickens's Uriah Heep, or with a colourless, ineffectual shrinking from challenges.

Yet 'meek' is an adjective that Jesus applies to himself (Mt. 11.29 in the King James translation); and the Jesus of the gospels, that forthright, stark and sometimes confrontational character who steps so vividly from the pages of the evangelists, is not particularly reminiscent of Uriah Heep, let alone of ineffectual shrinking from challenges. When Jesus calls himself 'meek' or 'humble' (*praus* in Greek), he is speaking, significantly, in the context of inviting people to lay their burdens on him: 'Come to me, all you that are weary and are carrying heavy burdens ... for I am gentle and humble in heart.' And this surely suggests that the 'meekness' about which he talks must be connected with a willingness to be open to the neighbour, not to push away the other, a willingness to share the vulnerability of the neighbour.

Meekness, then, might be reimagined as something to do with an attitude to others that is not self-abasing but simply alert to the reality of others, as Jesus declares that he is in those verses from Matthew 11. His humility is a capacity to be a place where others find rest. The humble person is the one who is not anxiously defended, not restless or tense over their status and safety, the person who is not anxious to hold, to keep control, but who simply occupies the place they occupy. And if that is what we are talking about here, a quality of stillness and alertness, it is possible to see how – as in some of the narrative about Jesus – anger can arise as a simple moment of passionate protest against pain, evil or deceit.[3]

(I can recall an experience with a former colleague, a person of quite exceptional calm and – in the best sense – self-possession, during a visit to Africa when we were held up for several hours in the middle of the night at a chaotically overcrowded airport, a context that might well have tested the patience of a desert father or mother. When, at about one o'clock in the morning, we and a crowd of local passengers had for the third or fourth time been taken out on to the tarmac and ordered back, my colleague stepped in front of a weeping mother with an understandably restless baby in her arms, and spoke firmly and just a bit sharply to the officious airport staff. I observed to her that on our return I would write to the airport and ask them to put up a plaque saying that AB *nearly* lost her temper here. People would come from all over the world to see just how bad it must be.)

Meekness as a habit of calm attentiveness, stillness, freedom from the fretting worry of keeping control, a stillness that allows others to feel welcome around you, can appear as something very different from the shrinking back that the word so easily suggests. Thinking back to our discussions in the last chapter, if anger is very much to do with the 'pushing out and pushing away' element in our psyche, 'meekness' in the sense of a welcoming stillness is the opposite of this. It is the dropping

38

away of the pushing, chest-beating style of response (remember the association of anger with the chest in Greek thought). And the blessedness of the meek, the blessedness of those who live in welcoming stillness, is the condition of those who will 'inherit the earth' simply because their spirit is one of receptivity: they are able to welcome truth, to welcome the neighbour; they welcome the world they live in, not needing always to be pushing outwards, battling, throwing up the defences. The earth is theirs because they are not obsessed about what is and isn't theirs: a theme that will come up in some of the other contexts we shall be looking at.

Anger is something with a good use, and Jesus himself uses it; but this 'good use' depends on its being the fruit of a truthful vision of what is damaged in us and our world. For us routinely sinful mortals, it is both useful and profoundly dangerous because it is so easy to delude ourselves that we are using it properly. And if we want to be delivered from using it improperly, self-indulgently, we need to keep asking who and what our anger serves, who it is for. At the same time, we need to go on inviting the grace of the Holy Spirit to make us still enough for the doors of vision and welcome to open and lead us to our 'inheritance', the state of things in which we are at home and able to make others at home.

If anger is something for which the monastic teachers have a slight soft spot, the same cannot be said of gluttony. It is significant that some lists of the passions, including Cassian's, begin with gluttony. The idea that Adam fell because of gluttony (wanting to eat what he did not need) is commonplace in the literature of the period. Gluttony is the craving for what is more than necessary, more than you need; and, as Cassian says, this can exhibit itself in a number of ways. Ironically, it can even show itself in the desire to be conspicuous for what you *don't* eat. If your eating is more about your desire to sustain a reputation for asceticism than the plain attention to the needs of your body, it has become a spiritual pitfall, another form of slavery to passion. Like all the teachers of the era, Cassian sees an asceticism that doesn't pay attention to what you actually need as being no less a problem than excessive greed. On gluttony, he has what you may find a rather startling passage referring to the sixteenth chapter of the prophet Ezekiel, which enumerates the sins of the people of Sodom and connects their destruction with 'excess of food and prosperous ease'.[4] For Ezekiel, the Sodomites are guilty of all kinds of social injustice – they oppress the poor and abuse the stranger. 'And why?' asks Cassian. Because they are slaves to gluttony. They are destroyed, says Cassian, not because of too much wine or too many other indulgences, but because of what the prophet simply calls 'a surfeit of bread'.[5] Not exactly the sin of Sodom as it has been commonly interpreted.

But, leaving aside this tantalizing hermeneutical byway, we can perhaps see how gluttony as understood by Cassian is yet another instance of slavery to passion as a kind of unreality, a failure to recognize what I actually am and what I actually need. And so we return to our basic theme: I rebel against being dependent, and so I resent being invited to think carefully about my *needs*. In consequence, either I set up a fantasy of myself as a giant of asceticism who can do without the ordinary necessities of life or I stuff myself full of what I don't actually need and don't truthfully want. I lose touch with something fundamental about my relationship with the world around me. Gluttony, as the spiritual tradition approaches it, is another way of losing touch with our *createdness*: so much comes back to this. We lose touch with what it is to be a created being, and so lose touch with the basic truth that we are because God is.

As we have noted, gluttony often features at or near the beginning of the lists of the eight passions; and there is a very strong tradition, going back as far as Origen in the third century, of setting Adam's gluttony in eating the forbidden fruit against Christ's fasting in the wilderness: Jesus' response to the Devil's temptation, that we do not live 'by bread alone, but by every word that proceeds from the mouth of God', is set over against Adam's greed. Christ recognizes that we live by the creative indwelling Word that gives food for body and spirit, by the self-giving life of God that is the centre of Jesus' own identity; in depending on this, we live, moment by moment, in the hand of God. But Adam, like Lucifer, wants to be something more than a created being; he is eager to lose touch with the ordinary needs and balances of creation, with the results that we see in our fallen, ravaged and exploited world. It is yet another reminder, if we need one, that the passions of the soul, as the tradition spells them out, are not simply a matter of our individual human qualities; they have to do with our relatedness to the rest of creation. Getting our relatedness wrong puts us out of kilter with the universe we're in and leads inexorably to the division between humanity and other creatures that is so alarmingly evident in the twenty-first century.

It's because of this relational dimension in coping with the passions that I want to link what is said about the passion of gluttonous consumption with 'hunger and thirst for justice' as its 'beatitudinal' counterpart. Those people are blessed, says Jesus, who are hungry and thirsty not simply for their own survival but for the well-being, the just balance, of the whole world God has made. It is as if Christ is saying to us that what we need to be authentically ourselves, the nourishment that will allow us to grow as we should, is the well-being of others, of our neighbours. We are as dependent for our life and flourishing on the well-being of our neighbours as we are on the food we eat.

We might remember Jesus in Chapter 4 of the Fourth Gospel saying, when the disciples come back from Shechem and see him talking to the Samaritan woman, 'I have food to eat that you do not know about.' What has Jesus been doing? Bringing a soul alive. He has been feeding with hope and vision an averagely confused and sinful member of the human race, the Samaritan woman of the story, and in feeding her, giving her life, he has been fed. The hunger and thirst which he exhibits at the beginning of this chapter, when he sits down by Jacob's well, is answered by the flourishing and releasing of the person he speaks with and serves. Justice has been done to her; something has been given to the woman that she needs for her life, and she in turn goes to break and share that bread with her own neighbours. 'Come and see the man who told me everything I ever did,' she cries, the wonderful, almost incoherent, good news that bursts from her as she rushes back to the city.

What we need in order to live in a balanced, 'reasonable' way within creation is the well-being and flourishing of our neighbours, justice being done to and for them. When we live untouched or uncaring in the midst of poverty, disease, violence, corruption and disaster, we starve. Our failure in giving to the neighbour becomes an injury to ourselves; we experience a famine of the soul as surely as the neighbour faces a famine of the body. 'Bread for myself is a material question, bread for my neighbour is a spiritual question,' said the Russian thinker Nikolai Berdyaev. It is the subtext we ought to read in every disaster or emergency appeal, in every reporting of poverty and pressure, near or far. Bread for my neighbour is a spiritual question.

So our hunger and thirst for justice, for God's righteousness, are a hunger and thirst that allow us to become what God wants, givers of God's gifts; and it is thus the opposite of the 'gluttony' that loses touch with our createdness, our connectedness with the neighbour and the world. Like the Lord, ministering to the Samaritan woman and finding food and drink in this encounter, so we in our passionate need for the life and well-being of the neighbour will be 'satisfied'. We shall receive what we need to be human.

These passions of anger and gluttony can be thought of as summing up the two basic energies we live with and the two basic kinds of distortion we are vulnerable to – the urge to push away defensively, and the urge to consume and absorb. In both, we seek to build up a self-oriented picture of ourselves; and both are healed as we reconnect with what we are as created lives, reconnect in the stillness of a proper humility, which, so far from being weak or evasive, is a profoundly robust anchorage for ourselves and others. As we connect with the need of the neighbour, we are brought back into the work of finding a 'just balance' for the whole universe. And the grace that leads us here is a grace that takes us into the heart of our nature, takes us back to where we belong in the hand of God; being what we are because of what God is. It is a grace that delivers us from the fretting, the resentment, the restlessness, the unreality, the posturing, the theatre of aggression and consumption. The 'blessed' persons of whom Jesus speaks are those who live in welcoming stillness yet are at the same time on fire with longing for the well-being of the neighbour and the healing of the world's hurts. Everything here points back to that central challenge of resisting the temptations of pride, the seductive pressure to imagine that we are not, after all, created and dependent beings. And here is the paradox, which we touched on briefly in the previous chapter, that becoming more creaturely, getting more deeply in touch with our createdness, is the way in which we more profoundly and fully come to share the life of the creator, the life of Christ himself.

4

AVARICE, LUST AND THE RISKS
OF MERCY

As we have seen already, the early monastic tradition recognizes that we are not required to think of our passions, as such, as being evil. The instinct for life and the consequent need to protect and nourish ourselves are part of what we are given in the fact of our createdness; the problem is what we do with them, what we train our instinct towards, what we allow to dominate and dictate our responses. This is where natural instinct turns to something very different. The passion of avarice, as described by Cassian, is presented very plainly as something unnatural. The root instincts of the soul, the aggressive and desirous passions, are at least natural; it's hard to imagine humanity without something like these instincts; but what exactly does it take to make us avaricious? Quite a lot of work, actually; and Cassian is mercilessly sharp about just how much *effort* we have to put into becoming avaricious.

We looked at gluttony in terms of a sort of losing touch with the basic createdness of our existence, whether by over-denial or over-indulgence, and avarice has something in common with that. But it is intriguing that the analysis offered by our texts of the passion of avarice is significantly different from what is said of ordinary greed. Two aspects need to be noted. First, avarice is seen as a longing for control – control over others, control over one's circumstances (present and future), control over one's image. You may think, says Cassian (and Evagrius had said much the same), that having many possessions might be a good thing because you would have a lot to give away, but be warned – behind this lies a desire that people will be indebted to you and revere your generosity.[1] And what exactly is this except another form of seeking control? I want people to be in my debt; I want to have a hold over them, to be in control of what people think of me. This is an initial problem with avarice. And the other problem is, very simply, that it represents a failure to trust the providence of God. Avarice arises from various sorts of fear: the fear of being at the mercy of other people's perceptions and other people's freedom, the fear of an unknown future that urges me to make sure I have resources for all crises and eventualities – a fear that can lead to unlimited avarice because I can never know what lies ahead.

What vanishes here is our confidence in the mercy of God, our belief in a God who holds us securely when we are not and cannot be in control, a God who (to underline it yet again) makes us to be what we are because God is who God is. In such a context, avarice is our ingenious effort to get around the fundamental riskiness of our situation because we do not really trust God to look after us. (You may recall the old anecdote of the man who is running from a tiger and comes to the edge of a cliff; he hangs on to a tuft of grass at the cliff edge, his legs dangling in mid-air, with the tiger looming over him and cries out, 'Is there anyone there?' A sympathetic voice from heaven replies, 'Yes, my son; let go.' There is a pause, and the man says, 'Is there anyone else there?') The tradition would have seen lack of trust as a manifestation of avarice, odd as this might sound, because it is about a refusal of the risks involved in hope for the future.

Wanting to be in charge of my own image, of how others perceive me, is probably one of the most troubling elements in all this – 'avariciously' grasping at how others see me, because it would be so much easier if we could all control what other people thought of us. But it is because of this worry about being at the mercy of what others think of us or see in us that we might link the passion of avarice with the beatitude of *mercy* as its gospel opposite. 'Blessed are the merciful; mercy will be shown to them': not an immediately obvious connection, but it may come into focus if we remember that mercy, forgiveness, can be a seriously risky affair. As Jesus speaks about it in the gospels, it is connected with the recognition that keeping myself safe in my own eye – which includes never yielding the moral high ground and the clear sense of what is due to me – leaves me profoundly *unsafe* in the eyes of God. Keeping myself safe in the ways we have been tracing is blocking off life: if life is always what we are *given*, not something we own, then the refusal to give life to another by seeking reconciliation and renewal of relationship is not only depriving someone else; it is also shutting out a channel by which life may come to me. Letting go of the urge to be right and the image of myself as someone to whom debts are always outstanding is at the heart of what mercy means. I don't 'stand on my rights'; I don't insist on what I have calculated is due to me; I don't defer any building of relationship until the scores are settled. Put like this, it may be easier to see the connection with avarice as a longing to keep others in my debt. Mercy scores a line through the whole language of debt.

This is why mercy is so consistently presented in both Hebrew and Christian Scripture – as indeed in Islam also – as an essential, unchanging attribute of divine life. One of the most striking images of redemption in the whole of Christian Scripture is Paul's language in his letter to the Colossians about God striking through the list of what we owe him and nailing it up in public on the cross, as someone might nail up a cancelled bill in a public place: an extraordinary metaphor, that the crucified body of Jesus on the cross is the certification of our debts to God being cleared. In the light of this, the language of debt and obligation, our own insistence on rights and claims, become embarrassingly unreal and empty.

But we have to add a clarification. This is not about denying the entire language of rights, brushing away all claims for just reparation, recommending to other people that they put up passively with injustice. We have already heard the call to be hungry and thirsty for justice; and the belief that human beings are created in God's image implies that reverence and love are the proper, the *just* response required. We are bound to work for a social order in which all may have a reasonable expectation of dignity and liberty, and we are bound to work at healing the long-term injuries that past violence and injustice have created (the legacies of racism and slave economies are at the moment rightly uppermost in the mind of many in the 'developed' world). But to put it like that is already to suggest how we might reconcile this with the critique of the debt economy. Chronic structural injustice means that some people are effectively prevented from *giving*, from having a part in the sharing of life and the building of community. To claim the freedom for this is something rather different from demanding the payment of debts in the ordinary sense; even talking about reparations for slavery is first and foremost recognizing the lasting damage done to others by a scandalous injustice and addressing that damage.

The critique of debt language in Christian Scripture is addressed to those who already have a disproportionate hold on power, those who are able to dictate the rules of a relationship and to preserve the imbalance within it. And it is also addressed – it must be said – to each of us to the extent that we cling to satisfying pictures of our personal rightness or entitlement, or to anxieties about preserving our secure privilege, independently of the task of creating a more genuinely mutual social world. It is essential that we think of what is 'due' to all creatures (non-human as well as human), the debt of respect and nurture that is owed; but this is to use the language of debt in a very different way from the clamorous insistence on what is owed to me in order that my comfort should not be challenged. Jesus himself, in his most vivid parable about debt (Mt. 18), depicts a slave whose immense debt to his royal master is written off and who then decides to exercise his own limited power in insisting, with threats and violence, on the payment of a small debt to himself: he has failed to grasp that his master has, paradoxically, paid him the debt of grace and respect and has not understood that, even with his limited power and security, he now has to show the same 'just' attention to someone even less powerful. The fact that he has been shown mercy is not a privilege that enables him to live without cost but a gift that enables him to create justice in his turn.

Mercy – letting go of the power we long for, letting go of the need for control, the need to be always the one who has the freedom to define others, always the one to whom something is owed, always the one who is the object of admiration for their generosity – is what stands over against avarice. Jesus tells his disciples that 'The kings of the gentiles exercise authority over them and their great men are called benefactors': a sharp and characteristic piece of irony. Here are all these potentates in the Roman political world of the day, dealing out life and death with a broad hand so that everyone is constantly reminded that they are controlled by a power they cannot challenge or hold to account – and they are adored and admired for it. Not so for you, says Jesus to his friends. And he himself demonstrates, again and again, how all of this language of indebtedness, and the tangled webs of status, power and deference associated with it, are irrelevant to the life of the Kingdom. Blessed are the merciful; mercy will be shown to them. Drop your own obsession with debt, control and all the rest of it, and you may find that another kind of relationship becomes possible – that essential Kingdom-shaped relationship which is mutual giving, mutual nourishing – that world of the Kingdom, into which the Beatitudes seek to introduce us.

When Cassian and his contemporaries turn to reflect on lust, they recognize that – as in the case of anger – there is something natural and unavoidable at the heart of it; the problem is not an 'evil' impulse but a painfully ludicrous distortion of something positive. As we have seen already at some points, *desire* as such is recognized by the tradition as natural. Cassian, in his discussion of the lusts of the flesh, says matter-of-factly that 'sensual' desire and pleasure are there from the beginning of our physical lives. Look at the baby at the breast; look at the child delighting in its body in all kinds of ways. Centuries before Freud, these observers of the human subject were able to connect sexuality with the infantile search for gratification. And there is nothing to worry about there. But as we 'mature', we do some very strange things with our desires. Cassian is clear that you cannot blame desire in itself, or the reality of bodily enjoyment and our search for this, for the distorted, selfish and confused habits that we develop any more, we might say, than, if you leave a knife around in the kitchen that's meant to cut cabbages, you can blame the person who left it there for a murder committed with that knife. There are inclinations that are bound up in our embodied life; this is what we are and who we are, and at that level there is nothing to be ashamed of.

Specifically sexual desire, says Cassian, is given to us for a perfectly straightforward reason. Like every other Christian in his age, he thinks it is entirely about procreation; and modern readers will undoubtedly want to argue the point and insist that something broader is involved in terms of building and sustaining life-giving relationships. But the argument still has force. There is a fundamentally creative and mutual or relational impulse that is thrown off balance when the only motivation I recognize is the urge that *I* be satisfied, as fully and as promptly as possible. This is the point at which we begin to speak of lust rather than desire. It is something that can apply to a great deal more than the body of another: it can relate to any kind of reduction of what is other to those aspects of it that promise gratification to me as an individual with no hint of real interconnection or mutuality. It can mean any action in which the dominant motive is that I be satisfied.

But to make full sense of this, we need to step back for a moment. The word 'desire' – *epithumia* in Greek – is one that appears in the Greek Old Testament in one particular context that gave it special significance. In the Book of Daniel, the visionary is addressed by one of his angelic visitants as 'Daniel, greatly beloved' (Dan. 10.11, 10.19). The Greek translators read an idiomatic Hebrew expression literally and rendered this as 'Daniel, man of desires' (*aner epithumion*). Clearly, so the Greek Christian theologians reasoned, to be described as a 'man of desires' by an angel is meant to be a compliment in this context. Daniel is being praised for having desires, and this encouraged the interpreters of the early Church to conclude that desire must be a good thing. The great fourth-century thinker Gregory of Nyssa, gives some serious attention to this;[2] and one notable feature of his work is his insistence on the role of desire in the life of discipleship. For Gregory, desire never leaves us, simply because there cannot be anything that finally satisfies us. We are so constituted that we are always in need of fulfilment, never attaining it in the sense of possessing what we most deeply need. If we are growing in spiritual maturity and discernment, what we desire is always to go on growing and to go on desiring. The mistake is to *want to stop wanting* – to desire to be satisfied so that I shall not have to desire any more, because I now have what before I lacked. I identify something, some object, which I believe will bring me a sense of greater completion: this will bring the fulfilment I lack, and when I have acquired it or mastered it, I don't need any longer to orient myself towards it. But for Gregory, our human nature is not like that: it is something constantly evolving towards a horizon never possessed, a depth never sounded, the triune life that is 'water to swim in, without ever travelling through it', in the image of the great Welsh hymn-writer Ann Griffiths.[3]

This leads Gregory to talk of heaven itself as an endless desiring – in the sense that there will always be more of God to discover and enjoy. We do not arrive in the Kingdom of God and enter into the experience of having got what we wanted – as if we could say that now we have 'enough' of God's loving presence. On the contrary: if we are truly 'men and women of desires', like Daniel, we shall never stop longing to love and be loved more and more. God's life is infinite, boundless, and so 'heaven' is a sinking deeper and deeper into an ocean that has no ocean floor. The goodness of 'desire' in this framework is the goodness of recognizing that we are always open to more; as finite beings faced with infinite life and joy, there is always going to be more to be discovered.

In this perspective we can see why our human desires can be both positive and negative. Positive desire is the longing to grow into more openness to a reality that is beyond the capacity of my own selfhood to digest or absorb. I am longing not for something to 'plug a gap' in my selfhood but for something that opens me up still further. A false or negative desire that in effect says, 'When I have acquired this or that, all will be well for me', both preserves a dangerous fiction about my individual self and its claims, and comes to regard the things of the environment as existing first and foremost in relation to me. Whether it is a person, a relationship, a state of life, a possession, whatever, the attitude that says, 'All will be well when I've got this' represents a deeply illusory picture of both self and world.

The point is made powerfully in Book 4 of St Augustine's *Confessions*, where the saint analyses, with his usual depth and subtlety, a moment from his adolescent years.[4] His closest friend dies unexpectedly, and Augustine meditates at length on his sense of utter disorientation and loss. He concludes that the trouble with his emotions through this period of grief was that he had been investing too much in this friend; his passionate devotion and companionship had in fact been a way of turning his friend into an adjunct to his own happiness and security. The friend was the one who 'completed' him, rather than a mysteriously inexhaustible other. And so, when the friend died, Augustine's deep and confused grief was a lament for the reduction in his own life. His inability to come to terms with his loss suggested – to use his own brilliantly evocative phrase – that he had failed to love his human friend *humaniter* – in a human way.

To love someone else simply as someone who 'plugs a gap', whose role is to complete you, is to treat them as less than human, to make their identity serve yours, instead of wondering at their difference, their mystery; and so it never allows your relationship with that mysterious otherness to lead you deeper into the ultimate mystery which is God. 'Lust' is something to do with that inhuman or dehumanizing desire that reduces the independent reality around you to mere functionality, a set of characteristics that will slot into the pre-existing space in your heart. And perhaps the deepest paradox Augustine points us to is the recognition that, when we project all this on to another item in the world, another thing, person or state of affairs, we both reduce them to less than they are and inflate them to a sort of godlike status as the final answer to our needs. The difficult and all-important truth is that the 'answer' to our human need and longing is the reality that is never exhausted, understood and possessed. To love 'humanly' is to accept that the person or thing loved is neither God nor a passive item for my ego to collect and use but a life that is genuinely other, existing in relation to the infinite love of God just as I do.

Can we then connect the passion of misconceived desire with the beatitude about 'purity of heart'? The pure in heart, says Jesus, will 'see God'. Instead of the short-term and self-oriented desires that are supposed to bring satisfaction moment by moment, we discover a lasting and single-minded longing to keep open to the truth, to keep open to the love and the reality that are God, recognizing that this longing can never be satisfied, over and done with. Purity of heart, said a great philosopher, is 'to will one thing':[5] purity of heart is what holds together all the diversity of our relationships and desires by connecting them to that single longing to be in touch with what is real, with the loving reality of God. Our purity of heart is discovering again and again, in this or that relationship, in this or that situation, what it is that opens out on to a deeper level of longing; instead of stopping or freezing our growth, fixing it at the level of temporary gratification.

It's a theme explored very illuminatingly in some of C. S. Lewis's writing. Lewis notes in his autobiographical reflections how, as a teenager, he'd first experienced what he called a sensation of joy that was inseparable from a sensation of yearning.[6] If *this* is wonderful, how much deeper must be the reality out of which it flows. At the very end of the *Chronicles of Narnia*, in the renewed world, the children are called 'further up and further in'. The landscape dissolves not into a fainter and more ethereal scene but into something more solid and real; that newly solid and real landscape in turn opens out to become yet more solid. At every stage something that is wonderful melts into something still more wonderful. 'Purity of heart' is being willing to go on making that journey single-mindedly – not despising and discarding what is along the way but recognizing a beauty that always urges us further, away from the mindset that looks for a static end to our wanting and reduces the world to the dimensions of what we currently think will give us a sense of worth.

The desire that merges finally into purity of heart is a desire *not to stop desiring*, a desire to be kept open to truth and loveliness, wherever it may be. It is the opposite of 'craving', the obsessive urge to possess ('When I've got that, I'll be happy'). The paradox is that, if you desire to keep on desiring, you can be happy now, not tomorrow. The person who says 'When I've got that, I'll be happy' is the person who puts off fulfilment or peace until they have acquired some object; and, as we all know, when this has been attained, there is always another all-important object to acquire. But if you say, 'My task, my destiny as a human being, is to have my heart constantly enlarged,' then today I am already being given the gift which will equip me for today and tomorrow; and tomorrow I shall be given the gift that'll equip me for the day after. I am growing steadily into the depth of God's mystery and God's beauty. This does not mean that I shall be spared any vulnerability to loss and pain; the beauty or joy of what is immediate to me and enriches me will bring pain if and when it is lost because it reminds me of the depth of my need – but also of the immensity of what is promised.

Avarice is the compulsion towards control, the urge to be in control now and to overcome the risks that come in an unknown future; lust is the attitude to things and people which treats them as stopgaps to resolve our short-term needs and shrinks the world to the dimensions of my urges and fantasies. Against both of these stands the risky openness of the Kingdom, the life of beatitude: the risk of mercy, forgetting about the security of knowing exactly what is owed to me, forgetting about the economy of debt; purity of heart, allowing God to unfold in every kind of desire the unifying thread that leads to the unlimited and undying and holds us back from enslaving one another to self-regarding fantasy.

5

ENVY, DESPAIR AND THE LIGHT OF HOPE

In these reflections we have been brought back repeatedly to the various ways in which the tradition insists that our humanity is incomplete, a 'work in progress', always finite and limited, always being fed, being enlarged by the limitless reality we are engaged with. We are brought back to the need to acknowledge and accept what and where we are as created beings, and to see that the *created* outworking of *uncreated* love is what this whole process is about (which is why the reality of Christ, the embodied form of the eternal unifying energy underlying all things, the divine Word, is always the context within which we understand the life of passion and blessedness).

We have seen how pride, in the sense of a radical refusal of dependence, is at the heart of our sicknesses. But the seventh of the passions at first sounds very like it: how do we clearly distinguish pride from 'self-esteem'? It may have been this problem that led Western teachers to replace this with 'envy' in the list, and we will see in a moment where the overlap is. But the basic difference between pride and self-esteem is that, if pride is a fundamental refusal of dependence, a fundamental refusal to see oneself in the hand of a loving God, self-esteem is something both more prosaic and something (in many ways) just as elusive to identify and difficult to eradicate.

Self-esteem, says Cassian, is something that can be nurtured in a wide variety of ways; as he rather acidly says (in effect), if you can't have spectacularly fashionable clothes, you can always have spectacularly shabby ones. The goal is the same, the maintenance of an aura of specialness. It is an impulse that connects with both anger and avarice as these have been analysed, an impulse tied in with the fear of the uncontrollability of others and the need to stay in charge of how you are seen. It involves the anxiety we've seen at work in avarice, the urge to be in control. It is not difficult to see how that maps on to envy. Behind these urges is the perennially attractive zero-sum game: if someone else is attracting admiration, and there is only a limited amount of admiration to go round, then if they are getting more of it, I am getting less. I have to make sure that I get my deserts (the debt economy once again) and am able to establish definitively what's due to me. If that means less for the other, that's the way the world is. Them or me.

This is so evidently at the root of virtually all major conflicts, social, national and political as much as personal. It assumes that there can never be 'enough to go round': if I have more, they have less; if they have more, I have less. It is not exactly absent from the life of the Church, which is odd, given that the Lord of the Church in the Gospels appears conspicuously as the one who refuses to work on the basis of zero-sum games. In the parable of the labourers in the vineyard, for example (Mt. 20), the owner of the vineyard makes if perfectly clear that, if he wants to give one apparently less deserving person the same amount of recognition and love that he gives to another with what looks like a better record, that is his business not ours, since he is obviously not constrained by lack of resources. Jesus' constant emphasis on God's absurd and prodigal love for the undeserving, God's insistence that loving them more doesn't mean loving you less – all this is something writ large on every page of the Gospels.

So the fears that drive self-esteem and envy, fears about whether I'm being deprived of what belongs by right to me when someone else is loved and valued, are countered by the acknowledgement of a

God who does not play that particular game, a God who in loving, even favouring, one does not neglect or deprive another – a God, indeed, who elects and favours one purely and simply so that others may be blessed (as with the calling of the Jewish people). In the economy of the Body of Christ, this becomes the ruling reality: every sign of love and grace bestowed on any person in the Church is given for the sake of all. The Church is truly the Church when the sanctity, the maturity, the freedom, the heroism of a holy person is understood not as some kind of threat or reproach to my own lack of those qualities but as gifts and resource for me, helping me to become a little less unholy, idle and unheroic than I might otherwise be – both directly, by way of example and inspiration, and less visibly through the self-forgetting prayer and intercession of those gifted by God with holiness.

And this can be linked with the blessing assured for the peacemakers. If we can ever get past the zero-sum mentality, what begins to happen is, precisely, peace – not peace in the sense of an armed truce or an uneasy neutralization but a true *shalom* in the biblical sense, a common and mutually assured well-being, poured out from God and shared among God's creatures. 'Blessed are the peacemakers, for they will be called children of God': children of God because they do what their father does, manifest as God's offspring because they do what their father wants. These are themes powerfully underlined by Jesus in the Fourth Gospel (look especially at 5.19–30). God will become recognizable in the world through the way in which his 'offspring' make visible the divine freedom to make peace in this expansive sense.

To make peace, to create space for God's harmonizing, peacemaking purpose to overflow in us in the giving and receiving of gifts, is what happens when we stop worrying whether someone is getting more of the cake than we are, whether improving the lot of others is going to undermine our own comfort. The Body of Christ is the model for human peace as shared, mutually assured, well-being not because in the Church as we know it everybody agrees with each other and serves the good of each other all the time (you may have noticed that this is rather less than obvious ...) but because the very nature of the Church as a 'supernatural' reality, the effect of the act of God, is in its essence a community in which the holiness of one is the gift of all, just as the pain of one is the pain of all.

If we can face and overcome the fear that we habitually try to cope with by taking refuge in self-esteem and envy, what happens is the space for peace. We become truly children of God in that we display where we come from, the eternal life that is itself a flow of gift and response. The peace that is active, mutually sustained well-being, that is ultimately the shared glorification of the creator by creation, this is what becomes possible if we are liberated from self-esteem and self-defence. Peace is ultimately a condition of cosmic praise. God has made the world to share the divine bliss; the sharing of that bliss means that harmonious joy arises from creation to the life of uncreated joy that is God, and this 'rising' and reflecting of created joy to uncreated is what we mean by praise.

But it is as if Jesus does not want to leave us at the end of the Beatitudes with any kind of illusion about how the blessed life will be experienced in the world as it is. There is a true promise, and we need to remember to distinguish it from deceptive promise. So Jesus turns finally to speak about the 'blessedness' of those who are here and now suffering for justice, those who are persecuted for the sake of the Kingdom. It is in some ways a startling and challenging conclusion; not so startling when we read the Beatitudes in the context of the whole story of Jesus' living and dying, but it is not hard to imagine a certain jolt in the transition for the first listeners, perhaps nodding approvingly at the promise to the peacemakers – and then, after a pause, hearing the sombre promise to those on whom suffering is inflicted because of their commitment to God's justice.

In the traditional Greek monastic list, the eighth passion is dejection or despair. The connection is not difficult to see: dejection is the absence of hope, the absence of a sense of the possible or the promising. As such, it is something that makes all the other passions impossible to deal with. Cassian – like many other commentators – says that the difference between Peter and Judas in the Gospel story is that Peter repents of his betrayal and Judas despairs. There is all the difference between the aching, tearing sorrow we may feel for our failures and the lethal absence of hope, the literally deadening despair that drives Judas to his tragic end. Despair of this kind is ultimately a matter of looking at our sins without any sense of *God's* perspective on sin: *we* have failed, *we* have once again demonstrated our worthlessness and our inability to change.

But what if we introduce God's point of view? In one respect, it is a ludicrously ambitious thing to do, yet it is what Jesus opens up to us – and it is surely part of what Paul means by speaking (1 Cor. 2.10–16) of how we have 'the mind of Christ'. God has not failed, has not changed; the divine sustaining love is what it always was and always will be. God's perspective on sin is the absolute willingness to forgive and heal.

Unless we can see our sin and our failure in that light, we shall indeed despair. Perhaps it is appropriate that we are invited to think about despair at the end of the list of passions, because if we have learned anything about our instinctual life in all these other contexts, we shall have seen again and again that what we are led back to is not just the recognition of who we are but the contemplation of who God is. And if we have really learned the lesson about who God is, we are less likely to fall victims to despair; we shall have learned that our point of view on our own failure is not the last word. Indeed, our point of view on the whole of our selfhood and our world is not the last word. Left to ourselves, how do we judge ourselves? Another iteration of the zero-sum game: we are likely to judge ourselves as either total successes or total failures, being in both cases totally wrong.

What God sees is the truth of our growing or failing to grow in the passage of time. God sees us as we are; and what we are answerable to is the truth that God sees. As we read in the First Letter of John (3.19–20), 'we will know that we are from the truth … whenever our hearts condemn us, for God is greater than our hearts.' And this is the link with the blessing of those who suffer persecution for the sake of justice. Those who are faithful to the Kingdom in the face of the worst that the world can do to them are demonstrating in the clearest way possible that the point of view of the human world is not the last word. There is a perspective on human affairs that is at an angle to what any of us has access to. My own view of myself, positive or negative, is not the last word, and neither is that of my critic or enemy. The person who is faithful under stress, attack and violence is declaring that they know there is another way of seeing, a truth not exhausted by what I or my enemies think, and a truth to which we are all accountable. This is why, from the beginning, narratives of martyrdom have mattered to Christians (and people of other faiths) as one of the resources that allow dejection to be resisted, that allow us to believe that the possibilities of our lives are not what we thought or feared. It is not so much that we are inspired to heroism, though we may be; it is simply that the range of human response to darkness, suffering or failure is revealed to be broader than we knew.

In any number of less dramatic ways than martyrdom, we shall in our own context have come across those who are able to live with attack, malice, self-doubt or failure without collapsing, those who are somehow able to recognize that it is God to whom they are answerable, who without undue drama remind us of the other point of view. The reality of grace comes across to us so often in those moments when we see, fleetingly but vividly, a situation in which someone appears to have a glimpse of 'God's point of view'. St Francis embracing the leper is a very obvious instance, but so is the sight of anyone humbled before the rejected and voiceless. It is in its way as significant as the sight of those facing unspeakable suffering, for the sake of the Kingdom.

(Some years ago, I listened, through an interpreter, in a stiflingly hot little office in Kolkata, to a woman from a north Indian village describing how she had watched her husband being hacked to death by a crowd when he refused to abjure his baptism. Another point of view – in one way so deeply assuring, even joyful, in another completely terrifying. If there is indeed another point of view with such commanding authority, why do I waste my time failing to get used to it? And what might the cost of *that* be?)

Those who stand firm in the face of persecution of whatever kind are the voices who speak into our despair, the ones who tell us that our perspective on the world, our standards, our judgements of ourselves, our neighbours' judgement of us and our judgement of our neighbours, is all relativized by the reality of the God who stands witness to the created world. This is not a conviction that guarantees security – quite the contrary; in itself it does not even tell us that there is healing beyond the mortal world (though other dimensions of our faith do). It is simply itself, the embodiment of another way of seeing. This is good news; when you hear it, says Jesus, be glad; if you suffer rejection and slander for believing it and him, 'jump for joy'. Easy to imagine him saying this with that wry and ironic note that is so often audible in the Gospels. Your reward is great, he says: your reward is *God* – the awareness of God's freedom not to be distracted or deflected from the divine nature and purpose by whatever the world does and whatever we do.

That is where the Beatitudes point us. Blessed are those who find themselves in tune with the freedom of God, and who find, by being in tune with that freedom of unbounded mercy and generosity, that they are able to see themselves, their confusions and conflicts, their passions and instincts, in the light of another perspective. All the work we undertake in understanding the life of our passions and instincts is a matter of keeping clear who the God is that we look to. We are sent back to the start, to the tension we thought about in terms of pride and poverty. Do we secretly believe we are our own creators? Or do we know that we are in the hand of God? Do we secretly believe we have the resources to make and remake ourselves alone? Or do we know that the rise and fall of our breathing is, literally and metaphorically, the business of God's Holy Spirit? Poverty of spirit, the acknowledgement of our dependence, is our richest resource, our final security; to know that we are creatures is the path to sharing the joy of the creator.

This is the joy which the risen Jesus opens for us. He has taken on and fully shared a humanity that is passionate and fragile; he knew instinct and emotion as we do, the strength, the tide flowing, of anger and desire, like the rest of us. But because, at the centre of Jesus' identity, there is the unbounded and unimaginable openness to God the Source, the Father, which is the life of the eternal Son, Jesus knows who he is as a human being in a way that others do not. Thus he is free to 'rework' the fabric of passionate humanity as a vehicle for the fullness of God. This is what he shares with us in his body, the Church – in the sacraments, in the tangible fellowship we share as believers, in the grace given to those who are blessed with the freedom to see and act in a way that is liberated not from passion itself but from the reactive and self-serving distortions of our instincts that generate the horrors of injustice and violence in our world. He has given us something of his 'mind', the mind of Christ, his point of view, through the gift we share of his Holy Spirit. Mysteriously – and very patchily for the most part – we can judge with his judgement. And as we go on reflecting on how our passions rise up, swirl around, try to take over, we need to have this life-giving judgement at work in us, a perspective on our inner tumults that allows us to say this is not all, this is not final. What *I* see is not all there is to see; and the life of the Spirit, clarifying my vision, is the constant gift of the risen Christ to me.

We began these reflections recollecting the imagery used by the monastic and liturgical tradition about the clarifying and illuminating effect of God's gift. When we talk about the light of the resurrection, this is what we are gesturing to. The light of the resurrection is not only what allows us to see ourselves a bit more clearly – which on its own is not especially good news. It is what allows us to see the entire landscape of God's creating activity in the radiance of Christ's presence in the Spirit. This landscape is, by God's grace, shown to us as our homeland; it is where we belong. And this is what the life of *apatheia*, the life of freedom from the tyranny of 'passion', is finally about; living in the joyful and grateful awareness of God's perspective on the creation God loves and transfigures; praying and labouring day by day for that inch-by-inch growth in clarity, freedom, charity; growing in the right kind of detachment that lets us see our muddled lives embraced and healed in Jesus, the author and the pioneer of our faithfulness.

PART TWO

6

TO STAND WHERE CHRIST STANDS

It might be as well to begin with a few thoughts about what Christian spirituality is not. It is an area that is constantly in need of a certain level of 'demythologizing', given that the word 'spiritual' has lately become strangely fashionable. The cultivation of 'spirit', the promotion of 'spiritual values' in our educational system, the sense that there is in our human life a rather elusive but probably quite important area that needs attention and that can be described as the 'spiritual' – all this encourages the idea that spirituality is primarily a way of developing a dimension of your humanity, exercising a neglected limb or muscle. It will easily be associated with therapies of various kinds, tactics for living harmoniously with the world (and with your own responses to the world), and it will therefore tend to see the world as presenting a set of difficulties to be overcome by the practice of wisdom of one sort or another. In such terms, it commands a good deal of tolerance (a prime spiritual virtue, or course), even from those who would regard religious commitment of a traditional kind as suspect.

There is nothing intrinsically wrong or stupid in this, and the notion that it might be a good idea to pay attention to how you live harmoniously in an environment that will pretty persistently hurt and frustrate you is a step forward. But if we want to understand the texts of the Christian spiritual tradition, we have to take several steps back from what might seem obvious these days about the nature of 'spirituality', since these contemporary categories will not take us very far; we shall frequently find ourselves baffled by the texts when they do not immediately or obviously reflect a wisdom about living in a complex environment. In contrast, they offer a radical redescription of that environment, in which the goals of human effort are not self-evident but need to be imagined and realized by a discipline wholly dependent on a number of fundamental beliefs about humanity and its maker. These are texts about how you come to be a native of a particular moral and imaginative world, so that you come to see and think yourself afresh. The task of learning techniques – not at all as alien to the Christian spiritual enterprise as some might imagine – is inseparable from that task of occupying a certain sort of place, grasping in a certain way where and who you are; and this place is specified not by any detached account of human beings in the universe but by a specific historical story and identity.

This becomes very clear if we look at what the very word 'spirit' means in the earliest Christian texts. Although St Paul can speak – so it seems – of a threefold structure to our human existence – body, soul and spirit (1 Thess. 5.23) – it is fairly clear from the rest of his work that 'spirit' is very far from being simply an area of human experience or a portion of the human constitution. As the major epistles make plain, living in or according to 'spirit' (and it is seldom clear whether this means simply and directly the Spirit of God or whether it includes ourselves as 'spiritual') is a designation of the entire set of our human relations, to God and each other and our environment. We are delivered from life according to 'flesh' which is defined consistently as life dominated by self-directed instinct – so that we may live 'no longer for ourselves' (2 Cor. 5.15), but live in *koinonia*: that is, in the kind of relations that are characterized by each person's passion for the other's good or welfare, and in the kind of relation to God that is characterized by the prayer Jesus himself prays, 'Abba, Father' (Rom. 8.5; Gal. 4.6). Thus is

81

our 'place' defined: we stand where Jesus stands as
Christian believers, and pray as Jesus prays; and
in standing in that place before God as 'Abba', we
share equally in Jesus' directedness towards the good
and the healing of the world. Placed together in the
place of Jesus, we are bound in *koinonia* towards
each other, seeing one another not as rivals but as
embodying a divine gift. Life in the spirit is life beyond
the boundaries erected between ourselves and each
other and ourselves and God (even, it is tempting to
add, between ourselves and ourselves, since the divine
Spirit, we are told, draws out of us what we did not
know we desired (Rom. 8.26)). Life in the spirit is
life that is decisively free from the obsessions of self-
justification, since the place of Jesus is the place of
the one to whom the Father has eternally said Yes;
there is no need to negotiate for space or argue for
favour and privilege, as it is always already given to
and through Jesus.

It is in this very basic Christian theological
perspective that we must look for the heart of
Christian spirituality, since the life of the spirit
cannot, in such a context, ever be an area of concern,
merely a dimension of a wider life; it is the life of
the believer, material and imaginative and desirous.
Which is why the study of 'spirituality' constantly
spills over into thinking about doctrine, ethics, art

and all sorts of things besides. The Christian writer dealing with spirituality is writing essentially about what it is for a whole human life to be lived in the 'place' defined by Jesus. In the rest of this chapter I want to look at some of the things that might be involved in occupying that place, particularly as they have been understood by some of the early and medieval writers in the tradition.

What makes the idea of the 'place' of Jesus Christ a complex thing to get hold of is that we have a narrative about Jesus at the heart of our faith as Christians; so that there are several moments and pictures that are associated with Jesus, and it is not possible to give a once-for-all static account of what is involved in the imitation of Christ. Jesus is a prophet and healer; Jesus prays with unique intimacy to God as Abba; Jesus is crucified and reviled; Jesus is raised to the heavenly places. And, for early Christian writers, there is a further dimension, in that Jesus is also the eternal Word of God made flesh; thus there is a kind of story to be told (an admittedly odd one) about the Word abandoning heavenly glory to become human, and a model of the eternal Word pouring himself out in adoration towards the Father and acting as the channel of the Father's creative love. How you talk about the life of the 'spirit' in such a connection will depend a lot on which story, which image, you settle on as central, or even (simply) which image works at this time for these purposes. If, then, we look, to begin with, at the theologies that dominated the schools of Alexandria in the second and third centuries, the theologies associated with Clement and Origen, we find at the centre of their account of the Christian life a set of ideas that most of us today would not instinctively associate with imitating Jesus, since we tend to focus on the historical prophet and healer whereas they consistently turned towards the eternal life of the Word, the Logos.

Jesus embodies a heavenly reality that is not quite on the same level as the ultimate source of everything, the one true God, yet is the way the one true God exercises his life. The Logos is, we could say, the shape of God's action, the channel through which the divine life flows as it acts. The divine life expresses itself as balance and harmony: the ultimate source is pure unity, but as this source acts and moves, it does so in a way that makes possible the coexistence of different realities in a harmonious, not a chaotic, relationship. For Origen, in particular, this expression of the divine will and action was eternal, always flowing out from God; and also it was itself a centre of action, in the sense that it was turned towards God in contemplation: the outflowing of divine action was balanced by the answering rhythm

84

of contemplative love returning to the one source. The true destiny of the creation is to be united with that answering rhythm: the life of the spirit is to be one with the Logos.

The human Jesus is the one created being that is in perfect alignment with the life of the Logos; he lives a perfectly 'reasonable' life. Such terminology is, of course, very strange to our ears, since we tend to think of reasonableness as if it meant simply being judicious or unemotional or prudent. It is a rather negative and very prosaic word. But for a writer such as Origen, and many of those who followed him, the reasonable life was one of absorbed bliss, contemplation of the beauty and simplicity of the divine life, freedom from the distractions of specific impressions drawn from the material world around; and freedom from 'passion', from the realm of reactive and self-oriented instinct and feeling. Limited, earthly images and aspirations drop away; the spirit returns to what it was made for, a life that simply reflects back to God with love God's own supremely active and unified nature.

The unbroken union of the Logos with Jesus makes it possible for us to have released in us the freedom to be our proper spiritual selves. But one implication of this, an implication that many generations of Christians have found problematic,

85

was that the concrete reality of Jesus' earthly life was of less spiritual interest in itself than the eternal life of the Logos which it embodied: the goal was not so much to imitate Jesus of Nazareth as to be at one with the heavenly Word. The narrative of Jesus was always pointing beyond itself, and to remain focused upon this would be to remain in a kind of slavery to the impressions of the world of the senses.

Here, then, the place of Jesus is finally the place of the Logos before the mystery of the Father, a mystery never fully penetrated or sounded. To arrive at this place requires an inner resolution of the tensions between the contemplative spirit and the pressures of emotion and instinct ('passion'), so that the spirit becomes free for the vision of God; and the goal of harmony with the Logos suggests also that our ultimate freedom is also an other-related balance with the rest of the created order – at least, the created order in its own inner truth and balance. In particular, the tradition stemming from Origen emphasized the importance of aligning your mind with the reasonable, ordered structure of a universe created by a rational, self-consistent God. Similarly, the journey to spiritual freedom must involve an alignment with the inner harmony of the Bible, which, like the universe as a whole, is the expression of a unified and rational wisdom under the guise of an apparently diverse and even conflict-ridden surface. The spiritual reader of the Bible discerns what is beneath the surface, the spiritual sense of the biblical narratives and injunctions, and learns to sit a bit light to the apparent (but potentially deceptive) surface difficulties.

The risks in this vision were clear to a good many early Christian thinkers; did all this not suggest too radical a schism between the spirit and its earthly casing? Did the spiritual reading of Scripture not risk making the real meaning of the Bible something quite divorced from the historical narratives? Did the emphasis on the heavenly Logos not draw our attention dangerously far from the fleshly Jesus who speaks to us as we are, beings of flesh and blood? There were those who, while deeply sympathetic to Origen and marked by his influence, struggled to avoid some of these dangers, in various ways. One of the most significant of these was the great fourth-century theologian Gregory of Nyssa, the most original and profound of that extraordinary group of thinkers, the Cappadocian Fathers, who, in the second half of the fourth century, established the classical vocabulary for thinking about God as Trinity. Gregory is careful to qualify anything that might lead us to think that the spirit is simply stronger and better than the body. The body itself is a kind of reflection of the spirit, on the one hand; and the spirit itself, because it is created, is always falling short of the full reality of God.

But there is a further important point: God is clearly understood by Gregory and his circle as eternally and necessarily Father, Son and Holy Spirit, not as a primordial transcendent Father whose mysteries are mediated to the lower regions by the Logos as a deputy. The Son and Spirit share fully the divine life. Thus it will not quite do simply to underline the goal of spiritual life as alignment with the Logos. Gregory can, in a way rather reminiscent of Origen, talk of how we take our stand on the 'rock' of Jesus Christ so as to see the divine mystery, but at the same time we are placed on the rock so that we can see God 'passing by'. Gregory is here interpreting the strange story about Moses in Exodus 33, where Moses asks to see God's glory, and God replies by promising to show Moses only his back as he passes by, since no one can see God's face and live. Gregory goes on to allude to the instruction of Christ in the Gospels that we are to follow him: you do not see the face of someone you are following. In other words, our vision of the glory of God is inseparable from the following of Jesus Christ; if we ask how Gregory understands being in the 'place' of Jesus, the answer is, paradoxically, that it is to be always moving in the direction of Jesus' movement, and moving not simply in our strength but being carried along by him.

This points up two very fundamental insights in Gregory's writing. He explores the Christian life in his greatest work on the subject, *The Life of Moses*, by reflection on the Exodus stories. We are delivered from slavery, slavery to selfishness and envy and so on, and then led into the desert; the journey reaches its climax at Mount Sinai, where Moses climbs up into the dense cloud at the mountain's peak, to meet God in darkness. So the life of the spirit is a life always in motion, never arriving at a final and satisfying level of comprehension; and it is a life that leads us into 'unknowing': the spirit, a created and limited reality, can never compass the whole of God's life, and the best we can hope for is to be swept up into the Son's journey towards the Father, his eternal and temporal pouring of his life into the life of the Father who eternally pours his life into the Son.

The emphasis here is subtly but distinctly different from what we find in Origen; Origen's picture sees the goal of Christian life as a vision cleared of all compromising elements of the diverse and distracting world; Gregory seems to envisage a goal that is both seeing and not-seeing, a vision that is never free of some element that we might call 'desire' – though he is agonizedly careful, in other works, in trying to find a way of saying this that will not suggest we are eternally dissatisfied or eternally yearning for something we lack that will give us gratification. The goal is, in a strange way, not being in the place of Jesus but being never quite in the place of Jesus, always being taken along the road that his life in eternity and in history defines. And this is why elsewhere Gregory is clear that the following of Jesus entails a perfectly practical kind of service to and acceptance of one another, and why in *The Life of Moses* he has so much to say about the destructive evil of envy in the Christian life – looking at one another rather than the Christ who goes ahead.

In stressing the element of darkness and unfinishedness in the Christian journey, Gregory is not, of course, inventing a new theme, though he is undoubtedly giving it a quite new degree of sophisticated exposition. Following Jesus, and finding his 'place' through darkness, might well be a summary of what earlier Christian generations thought about martyrdom; and for the first three centuries of the Church's life the most obvious and compelling model for sharing the place of Christ was that of martyrdom. The martyr's body is, in a very strong sense, the place where Christ is: the second-century slave girl Felicitas, anticipating her death in the arena, said that 'another will be in me who will suffer for me, as I shall suffer for him'; and it was another slave girl, Blandina, whose body crucified before the pagan mob is described as an image of her Lord. The martyr is the 'site' of holiness not because she or he is showing exemplary courage or whatever, but because Christ is substantially present in that suffering body, as surely as Christ is present in the bread and wine of the Eucharist. Indeed, it is just this parallel that is evoked by two famous texts about martyrdom. Ignatius, bishop of Antioch at the beginning of the second century, imagines his body being ground by the teeth of the animals in the arena so as to become bread for God's people. A few decades later, Ignatius' friend Polycarp, bishop of Smyrna, is brought into the arena for execution; before the fire is lit he prays, in words that are clearly meant to remind us of the eucharistic prayer he would have offered each Sunday. His body is the eucharistic offering where Christ will become present; and we should not be surprised when, from the midst of the flames, there comes a smell like that of bread baking.

But the literature about martyrs brings into focus one of the major problems in the life of the early Church. Where Christ is must be where authority is to be found; Ignatius makes it abundantly clear that his forthcoming sufferings for the sake of Christ give his decisions and commendations a special force, even in advance of the event. Later on, Christians who had been imprisoned and tortured for their faith could claim various kinds of authority on their release, authority that sometimes seemed to clash with that of the local hierarchy. And when the authority of the person who had suffered for their faith was increasingly replaced (after the days of persecution were over) by the authority of the holy ascetic, the person who had voluntarily undertaken suffering for the sake of Christ, some of the same tensions reappeared. This is not simply a problem of Church politics (though it is at least that, of course); in the light of what I have been arguing so far, it should be seen as a problem about where the place of Christ is to be identified most clearly. As recent research has emphasized, the tension was between recognizing Christ in the extraordinary achievement of the individual holy person and recognizing him in the corporate life, a life lived under visible systems of authority, of the Church. The sense in Ignatius or Polycarp of the extraordinary achievement of a martyr's death being a kind of sacramental offering to and for the entire Church shifted increasingly towards a more individualistic concentration on the charisma of the holy man or woman.

Both sides of this argument – which broke out very bitterly in Carthage in the mid-third century,

Alexandria in the early fourth century and Asia Minor in the mid-fourth century, to give only the most dramatic examples – had some theological rationale to appeal to. The place of Christ is nothing if not a personal site, something concrete in a particular biography and the particular location of a human body; yet the New Testament also makes it plain that the place of Christ is pre-eminently the common life, the *koinonia* of believers animated by the Holy Spirit. The difficult balance of these two factors left an abiding legacy to the Christian mind: the history of Christian 'spirituality' is full of instances of such a tension, of the double suspicion of individual charismatic authority and of unequivocal loyalty to historic authority.

Christianity, of all the major world religious traditions, has had perhaps the most consistently restless attitude towards authority – which tells us something about the deeply suspicious culture of Western modernity that springs from Christian questionings (for good and ill). As a good many recent scholars have insisted, understanding the Christian spiritual tradition can illuminate in remarkable ways our sense of our general cultural history. What Christians thought about their human integrity, the images they shaped of the self and its context, naturally moulded what could be thought about self and society as a whole – precisely because (to pick up an earlier point) they did not regard the spiritual as a privileged private area of feeling and self-cultivation.

One of the ways in which the Christian tradition shaped the sense of self for the cultures of the Mediterranean and northern Europe (and so also for North America) relates to another central theme in the quest for the peace of Christ. The self is deeply and indeed fundamentally 'erotic' – that is, a subject of desire. We have already seen how Gregory of Nyssa struggles with the problem of how to inscribe something like desire in the heart of his account of the self growing eternally Godwards. Augustine, in the next generation after Gregory, writing in a very different language (literally: in Latin, not Greek), pursued the same theme with unparalleled imagination and depth.

In what sense, though, is this to do with the place of Christ? It may seem, as we saw with Gregory, to be a bafflingly paradoxical identification of Christ's place with the place of his absence, the place where he has always been before but is no longer. Something of the explanation of this is developed by using not merely an erotic but a nuptial idiom to speak of our place in relation to Christ's. We are where he is not; but that place where he is not is also the place where he is bound to be as the lover or spouse of the created self.

To be in that place of Christ is to be Christ's 'other' in a relation as intimate as that of sexual union within the covenant of marriage; the object of an eternal and unfailing commitment, the object – in the bold language that Christian theologians did not shrink from using, despite its philosophical problems – of divine 'desire'.

The notion that Christ is the bridegroom of the Christian community is, of course, already there in the New Testament, where the ancient imagery of God as the husband of the people of Israel was taken up and transferred to God in Christ and the Israel of the Church; Ephesians and Revelation both witness eloquently to this usage. Origen seems to have been the first to offer a systematic interpretation of the Song of Songs in terms of Christ's love for the individual spirit and for the Church; and Gregory of Nyssa develops this a good deal further. In the Middle Ages, Bernard of Clairvaux's sermons on the Song furnish a classical example of how this exegesis blossomed, sometimes with what is to modern eyes a startling explicitness of erotic imagery.

But its most sophisticated development is probably in St John of the Cross in the sixteenth century. John's poetry, in particular, plays with the figures of erotic absence and erotic enjoyment in order to bring into focus the paradoxes of being where Jesus is and where Jesus is not. 'The beloved' has been present – not only in the world at large (as the one who creates and orders it) but also as lover, as one who has been enjoyed. The created self is 'wounded' as a result of this encounter: virginity is lost, the self-containment of the fallen creature is breached, joy is offered and briefly tasted, and then there is withdrawal and absence. Yet (as John's theological commentaries on the poetry amplify) the spirit's experience in absence, in the darkness of not knowing who or what it is when deprived of the erotic affirmation given by the Saviour, confirms the spirit more deeply in the place of a Christ whose work reaches its climax in the experience of absence – of desire confronted with inescapable death.

Christ's reduction to nothing in the inner and outer agony of the cross is what makes sense of the experience of the spirit in the anguish of dereliction; in that absence, the spirit is transformed to be more abidingly like Christ, its desire becoming more and more nothing but the utterly expectant, utterly hospitable openness of love such as exists eternally between the Father and the Word in the Spirit. The imagery of John's *Living Flame of Love* presupposes that the Holy Spirit as the agency of God transfiguring the spirit into divinity consumes the desire for specific worldly spiritual gratifications in order to make the spirit burn with the selfless desire of God for God (a paradoxical enough formulation, I know, but the only one that can quite express the radicality of what John is evoking).

Like his friend and directee Teresa, John believes that the place of Christ is the place of incarnation – that is, God's dispossession of divine security of distance in order to be entirely present in the world of flesh and blood as a fleshly agent, suffering and dying as we do. Much of Teresa's discussion of her 'mystical' experience comes down, finally, to the affirmation of a new rooting in the reality of the present human moment before God; the huge disruptions of her emotional turmoil, her visions and communications, serve ultimately to return her as a displaced, dispossessed person to the present, to being a place where the hospitable openness of God's love as realized definitively in the incarnation of God the Son is humanly specific.

John and Teresa experience and construct the process of dispossession in distinct ways, John always being more wary of the dramatic and tangible intrusions of grace in the physical experience of the believer, Teresa retaining a fascination (albeit, in the long run, a chastened fascination) with the extraordinary and preternatural. But they agree in looking finally to Christ as the defining shape of their own journeys. For John it is the passage to and through the 'night of the spirit', the final stripping away of all the systems and external reference points by which we seek to define ourselves, that brings us to where Christ is, as the intimate and inseparable other who can share his own intimate and inseparable otherness-in-love to the Father. For Teresa it is the dizzying upheavals of God's insistent love, sensed in body and spirit, that shake out our own conviction that we are in charge and lead us to be identified with the movement of the Word from the Father into the heart of the world (where in fact the Father already is, waiting expectantly for the Son to return to him).

Between them, the Spanish Carmelites give an unprecedentedly consistent reading of the life of the spirit in terms of conformation to Christ incarnate. It is a pity that they have come to be seen as of interest to students of the 'abnormal' in religious experience – Teresa, in particular – as if they were primarily interested in odd things happening to a privileged minority. Their own sense of what they were was clearly much more that they were seeking to grasp what was involved in being a baptized Christian in a serious way. They are, of course – as people of an age that was getting more and more interested in biography, in individual records of change and growth – far more closely focused on the specifics of the self than most of their precursors (Teresa especially); but it is important not to think that their agenda was different in kind from that of their medieval and patristic ancestors.

A brief introductory note such as this cannot pretend to cover the whole range of the literature of classical Christian spirituality. What I hope it may do is to offer an interpretative pattern for reading other texts, a set of questions that might be worth asking. As I said at the beginning of this chapter, if we approach Christian texts from any period before the nineteenth century with the primary question in our minds, 'What subjective experience are they trying to convey?', we shall be disappointed. We are so often encouraged to look for records of 'mystical experience' that we may miss what is most distinctive in what we read; we shall focus on phrases that suggest the sort of experience we think religious people ought to be having (encounters with the transcendent, feelings of absorption or whatever), and we shall overlook the ways in which a text works to provide a broad imaginative territory in which the particular reader is letting himself or herself be defined afresh – how they are letting themselves be converted, if you like. This means that a good reading of a classical text in this area will always be one that attends to the entire rhythm of its argument and the detail of its imagery. The question is: 'What does this writer want me to see? What of my own story: am I being invited to retell or recast it in the light of the way the text presents the story of God's action in Jesus Christ?'

As has been indicated, some of these ways will be very odd to us; most of us will not start with much sense of what meditation on the eternal Logos might have meant for an Alexandrian ascetic in the third Christian century. We may find Gregory of Nyssa on the imitation of the human compassion or even the divine kenosis of Christ more approachable, closer to a twentieth-century understanding of Christlikeness. But the underlying issue is the same; given belief in a Saviour who is both human and eternally active towards and on behalf of the divine source of all, no one category is going to exhaust what might be said about what it is to be where he is. Even without the complex development that increasingly understood being with Christ as being with him in his absence or otherness, it could never have been possible to define Christ's place in terms of one graspable image or ideal.

Christian writers are constantly having the wrong categories reconstructed by the alarming plurality of images of Christ generated by their theological and narrative heritage. And so far from this suggesting to them any kind of radical pluralism or relativism in their theologizing, they concluded that they needed a theological framework spacious enough to allow for such a bewildering multiplicity, a framework as broad as the whole discourse of God and of humanity. The point has been made often enough, but it is worth reiterating: the strains of classical theological language are in substantial part due to the scope of these redefinitions of God and the human that insistently edged into Christian speech through the corporate experiences of worship and mission.

7

EARLY CHRISTIAN WRITING

The writings that survive from the first three centuries of Christianity are mostly what one twentieth-century scholar of religion called 'death-cell philosophy': that is, they represent the kind of thinking that is done under extreme pressure, when what you say or think has a genuine life-or-death importance. Gregory Dix, an Anglican monk writing 80 or so years ago about the worship of the early Church, in one of the most vivid passages in his great work of 1945, *The Shape of the Liturgy*, imagined what it would be like to attend the Lord's Supper in second-century Rome by recreating the experience in terms of twentieth-century London. He takes the descriptions of worship from texts such as the so-called 'Teaching of the Twelve Apostles', the 'Didache', probably the most ancient account of worship outside the New Testament, and the 'Apostolic Tradition' from the second century, and translates them into the landscape of modern

England. A grocer from the unfashionable suburbs slips through the back door of a wealthy brother's house in Kensington at the crack of dawn, to share in the breaking of bread in the drawing room – a brief, quiet event, overshadowed by the knowledge that if you were discovered you could face at least penal servitude for life, and very likely worse. Any Christian in this period knew that, even if things were relatively peaceful for the time being, it was always possible that a suspicious government would crack down. Dix describes how the 'deacons', the ministers who looked after the doors, would be charged with scrutinizing everyone who came in very carefully; you'd need to know who your companions were if your life might depend on them.

The suspicions were well founded in one sense. If you look at the eyewitness accounts of martyrdom in these early centuries – documents such as the wonderful record of the martyrs of Scilla in north Africa in 180 CE – you can see what the real issue was. These Christians, most of them probably domestic slaves, have to explain to the magistrate that they are quite happy to pray for the imperial state, even to pay taxes, but that they cannot accept that the state has the right to absolute allegiance, to religious worship. They have another loyalty – which means not that they are working to overthrow the administration but that they will not comply with the state's demands in certain respects. They will not give religious adoration to the emperor; and, as we know from some other texts, they will not serve in the Roman army. They ask from the state what had been very reluctantly conceded to the Jews as an ethnic group – the right to be exempt from the religious requirements of the state. What makes their demand new and shocking is that it is not made on the basis of any ethnic identity but on the bare fact of conviction and conscience. For the first time in human history, individuals deny the state any right to override their beliefs; they claim for themselves the liberty to define the limits of their political loyalty, to test that loyalty by spiritual and ethical standards.

That is why the early Christian movement was so threatening – and so simply baffling – to the Roman authorities. It was not a revolutionary movement in the sense that it was trying to change the government. Its challenge was more serious: it was the claim to hold any and every government to account, to test its integrity and to give and withhold compliance accordingly. But it would be wrong to think of this as we are tempted to do in our era in terms of individual conscience as we now see it. It was about the right of a community to set its own standards of spiritual truthfulness and to form its members in the light of what it believed to have been given to them by a higher authority than the empire.

The core of the problem was that these early Christians believed that if Jesus of Nazareth was 'Lord', no one else could be Lord over him, and no one else could therefore overrule his authority. We use the word 'Lord' these days mostly in a rather unthinking religious context, as a sort of devotional flourish; for a Roman, it meant the person who made the decisions you had to abide by, from the master of a slave in the household to the emperor himself. To speak of Jesus as 'King of Kings and Lord of Lords' was to say that his decisions – his 'policy', you could almost say – could not be overridden by anyone, so that you might have to disobey a 'Lord' in our society in order to obey the one true Master of all – the one who used no violence in enforcing his decisions but was all the more unanswerable an authority because of that. He alone needed no reinforcement, no power, to overcome external threats or rivals.

So early Christianity was, on the one hand, a deeply political community, posing a very specific challenge to the state by saying that the state was a provisional reality – deserving of respect and routine compliance in the ordinary affairs of social life but having no ultimate claim. But on the other, it was a movement fascinated by the intellectual implications of this as well. Because if Jesus was 'Lord', and if God needed no force to defend his authority against rivals, the extraordinary implication was that Jesus' 'policy' was God's, that Jesus shared without qualification the Wisdom of God and the self-sufficiency of God – that's to say, he depended on nothing other and nothing less than God for being who he was. As early as the beginning of the second century we find the martyred bishop Ignatius from Antioch calling Jesus 'God' – because he needed no defence against rivals, and so was free to take on himself the burden of human suffering without fearing that he would be crushed or destroyed by it. And because of his own freedom in the face of appalling suffering he could make it possible for believers in him to face their own suffering with the same resolution and steadiness. What Ignatius called 'the passion of my God' became a gift to believers confronting those terrible risks that Gregory Dix brought alive so vividly in his study of early worshipping life.

The theology of the early centuries thus comes very directly out of this one great central conviction about political authority: if Jesus is Lord, no one else ultimately is, and so those who belong with Jesus, who share his life through the common life of the worshipping community, have a solidarity and a loyalty that goes beyond the chance identity of national or political life; and the first claim on their loyalty is the living out of the life of Jesus, which is also the life of God – a life that needs no defence and so has no function for violence and coercion. God, says Clement of Alexandria in the late second century, shows his love supremely in the fact that he loves people who have no 'natural' claim on him. Humans love largely because of fellow-feeling, but God's love is such that it never depends on just having something in common. The creator has in one sense nothing in common with his creation – how could he? But he is completely free to exercise his essential being, which is love, wherever he wills. And this teaches us that we too must learn to love beyond the boundaries of common interest and natural sympathy and, like God, love those who don't seem to have anything in common with us.

Here's one of the paradoxes of early Christian thought. It's really deeply rooted in intense, mutual, disciplined community life but at the same time insists on universal compassion and universal sympathy. And, so far from the theology of the early Church being an eccentric diversion from the real business of mutual love and generous service, it is possible to see that the doctrines of God's eternity and unchangeable consistency, the doctrine of Jesus' full participation in the divine life and ultimately the doctrine that

Christians came to call the divine Trinity and much more all derive pretty directly from reflection on the implications of saying that Jesus is truly the supreme authority and that he exhibits exactly the same liberty to love indiscriminately as does God himself. Jesus is the earthly face of an eternal love between Father, Son and Spirit. And when the early theologians write, as they often do, about how Christians are given a share in the divine life or the divine nature – language that can sound a bit shocking to modern believers – what they mean is simply that being in the Body of Christ, in the community of baptized believers, gives us the freedom to love God the Father as Jesus loves him, through the gift of the Holy Spirit, and so too to love the world with the unquestioning generosity of God, never restricting ourselves to love those who are familiar to us and are like us.

Writers on the life of prayer in this period – above all, the great Origen of Alexandria, who taught and wrote in the first half of the third century – associated Christian identity with freedom, the freedom to call God 'Father' and Jesus 'Lord', as Origen puts it; which is also, for him, a freedom from what he calls (confusingly to our ears) 'passion'. This doesn't mean that Christians should have no emotions; it does mean that they should be free from reactive, unthinking feelings that dictate their responses to people and things. Our response to the world around must be rooted in a renewal of our minds, seeing through the superficial differences to recognize God's presence and purpose in all persons and things.

And for all these great figures there were blindingly obvious practical implications for how we treat each other – implications about forgiveness and respect, about the urgent need to deal with poverty and suffering, about stepping back from the institutions of the state, especially the army. None of this was fully encoded in rules; but the Church expected people to be able to draw the obvious conclusions from the simple starting point of living under a new authority. We know that there were Christian soldiers in those centuries, but we know too that the community in general would never settle happily with the idea that Christians should bear arms. Origen is one of the many who could not be reconciled to that idea. And even when things were beginning to change drastically in the fourth century, with a Christian emperor who was increasingly sounding like his non-Christian predecessors, you'll find figures like Martin of Tours in France, who discover that when they are converted they can't bring themselves to carry on as soldiers. Even the formidable Augustine of Hippo at the beginning of the fifth century – famous as the man who first outlined the conditions for a 'just war' – is crystal clear that, while he thinks Christians may take part in defensive war to protect the weak, there is never any case for thinking that we should try to defend the gospel by war; at best it's an emergency measure. It's a pity that this side of Augustine's thought was largely overlooked by people eager to make him an ally of just those imperial military myths that he was so regularly scathing about.

Because we have to admit that by the fifth century the Church *was* looking different. Having become legal at the beginning of the fourth century, it steadily became more and more involved with the power of the state and was seen as giving legitimacy to the emperor. Those who argued for this were not wicked people who were simply hypnotized by power and influence (though no doubt some had their temptations). They thought that divine Providence had at last put an end to their cruel sufferings and provided them with an ally in the Christian emperor. Augustine is one of those who disagreed strongly with this, but not many took up his approach. For most, it was simply easier to believe that God had brought human history nearer its fulfilment by converting the power of the state. And it was when all this was going on that some serious Christians started moving away from cities and towns and becoming monks in the deserts of Egypt and Syria – so that they could reconstruct the life of the first believers in Jerusalem, sharing their property and living in simplicity.

For many centuries, indeed, the life of the monks was described as the 'apostolic' life. And originally it was a life for laypeople, not clergy; those who became monks were eager to escape from the hierarchy of the Church as much as the hierarchy of the state. In the sermons and stories that were developed in this setting, the same strong lines were worked out as we find in earlier writing: the common life of Christians must display the same characteristics as the life of the Lord, in unquestioning compassion and mercy, in generosity and simplicity and a refusal to defend oneself or compare oneself with others.

Of course, many of the assumptions made by the early Christians are not likely to be exactly ours – notably the very high valuation given to the single life rather than the family, though there are some who write eloquently on the latter as well. But the point I am looking to underline is that this was a period when the great central theme of Christian existence was how to live in such a way that it became clear where your loyalty lay – because this was the best way of witnessing to a God whose eternal life was utterly free from completion and conflict. The experience of a new way of living in community prompted theological questioning; the theological clarifications reinforced and deepened the sense of the priorities and imperatives for the community. You might say that the living out of the love of Jesus pressed believers to think harder about exactly where that love sprang from in the heart of God; and this thinking about the nature of God's very heart made it plain that the love made possible by Jesus was, quite simply, the most real and thus the most authoritative thing in the universe (and beyond it). It's perhaps not an accident that in the fourth century the most ardent defender of the divine dignity of Christ – Athanasius, bishop in Alexandria – was also the most courageous opponent of imperial authority when he deemed it necessary.

One of the lasting legacies of the early Church, then, is the recognition that doctrine and prayer and ethics don't exist in tidy separate compartments: each one shapes the others. And in the Church in any age, we should not be too surprised if we become hazy about our doctrine at a time when we are less clear about our priorities as a community, or that we become less passionate about service, forgiveness and peace when we have stopped thinking clearly about the true and eternal character of God. We don't have to be uncritical of the theologians and others in that early period. But what they have to offer us is a clear message about how Christian identity is always bound to be a claim to a 'citizenship' that is deeper and more universal than any human society can provide. Christians are always going to be living at an angle to the mainstream – not claiming a glib moral superiority but simply insisting that they 'march to a different drum', as some writers have put it, and that this is a consequence of recognizing final and unsurpassable authority in the living and dying of Jesus of Nazareth as the one who has the right and the liberty to tell us what is real and true in the universe.

It does not mean that the Church is now locked in a violent contest with state or society, that it is struggling for supremacy. That is the greatest mistake we could possibly make. If Christ is who we believe he is, there is never any need for struggle; nothing will make him less real or true. Insofar as there is a struggle, it is with our own willingness to let other authorities overrule Christ. In the early Church, that was a literal life-and-death matter – and it still is for Christians in some parts of the world today. For most of us the consequences are less dramatic, but the challenge is still there. Our faith is still a 'death-cell philosophy', certainly in a world that confuses 'life' with victory, prosperity, security at the expense of others. We know better what life really is – what must be let go of in order for it to flourish, what astonishing gifts are opened up for those who find the courage to step beyond what is conventionally and religiously taken for granted. And if the struggle is hard – as it is, even if we are not here and now threatened with martyrdom – there is all the more need for communities of believers trying to live out the radical imperatives – communities of monastic discipline in the old way, new communities focused on peace and the disciplines of non-violence. We can't do any of this as isolated individuals with an interior religiousness; we need the concrete reality of Christ's corporate Body, nourished by his Supper.

The thinking of the Christians of those first few centuries – their letters, their sermons, their forms of worship, even sometimes their fierce arguments about doctrine – shows us how talking of God and living in obedience to God are closely interwoven. For them, theology was not a luxury or an academic affair; it was their way of seeing more clearly what their way of life implied. That integrated sense of mind and will and heart exploring together is something we can still learn from these great figures, who often at the greatest personal risk discovered with joy what Christ asked of them and discovered with surprise what they were capable of in response. Reason enough for reading them again with eagerness and enthusiasm.

AUTHOR'S NOTE

The texts in Part 2 are lightly edited from two published pieces, 'What is Christian Spirituality?' in Ralph Waller and Benedicta Ward, SLG, ed., *Introduction to Christian Spirituality*, London, SPCK 1999, and the Introduction to *The Two Ways: The Early Christian Vision of Discipleship from the Didache and the Shepherd of Hermas*, Walden, NY and Robertsbridge UK, Plough Publications 2018.

NOTES

INTRODUCTION: A TRADITION FOR
LEARNING FREEDOM

1 References here are mostly to the great anthology of classic texts on spiritual maturity from the Eastern Christian world assembled in eighteenth-century Greece under the title of the *Philokalia* ('The Love of the Good/Beautiful'), translated in five volumes by G. E. H. Palmer, Philip Sherrard and Kallistos Ware (London: Faber and Faber, 1979–2023).

2 For example, *Philokalia* I, p. 307.

3 For example, *Philokalia* I, pp. 53, 62; *Philokalia* II, pp. 23, 317.

4 For example, *Philokalia* II, pp. 79, 314 and pp. 103–4, underline the way in which *apatheia* allows a true valuation of all things, a universal love and respect that is free from acquisitiveness.

5 *Philokalia* I, p. 285. Notice here the importance of calling on Jesus (Diadochos is one of the earliest writers to commend the repeated invocation of the name of Jesus as foundational for contemplative focus in prayer), and the importance of the idea that our actual physical perception is made keener and clearer by inner liberation (compare, for example, p. 259).

6 See Evagrius, 'On Thoughts', Chapter 8, in A. M. Casiday, *Evagrius Ponticus* (London: Routledge, 2006), pp. 95–6.

7 Teresa of Ávila, *The Interior Castle*, in *The Collected Work of St Teresa of Avila*, translated by Kieran Kavanaugh and Otilio Rodriguez (Washington, DC: Institute of Carmelite Studies, 1980), III.2, pp. 309–15.

8 See, for example, *The Interior Castle* I, pp. 331–2; II, pp. 277–8, 284, 293.

9 The image is found in Plato's dialogue the *Phaedrus*, and recurs in both Christian and non-Christian discussion of the human subject in the early centuries of the Christian era. See below, Chapter 4, n. 2.

10 Cf n. 3 above.

1. Mapping the Passions of the Soul

1 There are some helpful insights in Richard Sorabji, *Emotion and Peace of Mind: From Stoic Agitation to Christian Temptation* (Oxford: Duckworth, 2000), especially Chapters 22 and 23.

2 'On Watchfulness and Holiness'; for the analysis of temptation, see *Philokalia* I, pp. 170–71, and compare the slightly different but not inconsistent account given by Mark the Ascetic, *Philokalia* I, pp. 119–20.

3 *Philokalia* I, pp. 38 ff. (extracted from the longer texts *On Thoughts*: see Casiday, *Evagrius Ponticus*, pp. 91 ff.).

4 For Evagrius's listing, see his *Praktikos,* translated by John Eudes Bamberger (Kalamazoo, MI: Cistercian Publications, 1981), sections 6–14, pp. 16–20.

5 The text entitled 'On the Eight Vices' (*Philokalia* I, pp. 73–93) is a compilation from Cassian's *Institutes*, Books V–XII; there is another substantial treatment in his *Conferences*, Book V. Angela Tilby, *The Seven Deadly Sins: Their Origin in the Spiritual Teaching of Evagrius the Hermit* (London: SPCK, 2009), especially pp. 63–174, is helpful, and usefully traces (pp. 19–29) how the original eight 'thoughts' turn into seven 'sins'.

6 As, for example, in 'On Prayer', *Philokalia* I, pp. 58, 63–4.

7 For example, *Philokalia* I, p. 75: 'We must not therefore expend all our effort in bodily fasting.'

8 *Philokalia* I, p. 284.

9 *Philokalia* I, p. 307.

2. PRIDE, LISTLESSNESS AND THE TRUTH OF DEPENDENCE

1 *Philokalia* I, p. 92.

2 *Praktikos* 12, pp. 18–19.

3. ANGER, GLUTTONY AND THE GRACE OF POVERTY

1 For example, *Philokalia* I, pp. 22, 47, 168.

2 *Mary, Mother of Sorrows, Mother of Defiance* (Maryknoll, NY: Orbis Books, 1993).

3 As in the best attested reading of Mark 1.41, where Jesus is described as reacting with 'anger' to the leper's appeal to be healed.

4 Ezekiel 16.49: 'This was the guilt of your sister Sodom: she and her daughters had pride, excess of food, and prosperous ease, but did not aid the poor and needy.'

5 *Philokalia* I, p. 74.

4. AVARICE, LUST AND THE RISKS OF MERCY

1 *Philokalia* I, pp. 80–81.

2 In his work *On the Soul and the Resurrection,* a dialogue with his sister Macrina. This is one of those texts that alludes to Plato's metaphor of the chariot with its difficult-to-handle horses; Macrina is critical of the usefulness of Plato's model, but strongly affirming about the importance of desire properly understood.

3 'Dŵr i'w nofio heb fynd trwyddo', from her hymn beginning 'Bererin llesg gan rym y stormydd'.

4 *Confessions* IV.iv(7)–vii(12).

5 Søren Kierkegaard, *Purity of Heart Is to Will One Thing* (London: Collins, 1961).

6 C. S. Lewis, *Surprised by Joy: The Shape of My Early Life* (London: Geoffrey Bles, 1955).

INDEX OF NAMES